OTHER BOOKS BY JOHN C. BENNETT

Christianity and Our World

Social Salvation

CHRISTIAN REALISM

Christian Realism

by

John C. Bennett

New York

CHARLES SCRIBNER'S SONS

1941

Copyright, 1941, by
CHARLES SCRIBNER'S SONS

Printed in the United States of America

All rights reserved. No part of this book may be reproduced in any form without the permission of Charles Scribner's Sons

A

To

A. M. B.

PREFACE

THIS BOOK is an attempt to think through some of the most important problems of Christian life and thought in the light of insights which have come from recent developments in theology and in the light of the events that haunt our minds. The first chapter is a diagnosis of the existing situation and the chapters that follow are essays in theology. It is no longer necessary to apologize for the use of the word "theology" as theology is an area of thought that is extraordinarily relevant to the most urgent issues of our time. The position presented in this book will be difficult to label. Some liberals will regard the book as corrupted by what they call "neo-supernaturalism" or "neo-orthodoxy." Those whose rebellion against liberalism is most complete will see in it merely a different version of liberalism. I write as a liberal who tries to take seriously the contribution of such thinkers as Barth, Brunner, and Reinhold Niebuhr; and as a Congregationalist who believes in the central importance of the ecumenical Church.

The immediate occasion for the publication of this book is that I was asked to deliver the Council Lectures at the General Council of Congregational Christian Churches in August, 1940. I am most grateful to Doctor Douglas Horton and the other officers of the General Council for the stimulus and encouragement that were provided by their invitation. The original lectures have been largely rewritten and they have been very much expanded for publication.

The first chapter is the one most influenced by events since the invasion of the Low Countries. May it soon be out of date! As the book goes to press the situation seems more open and hopeful than it did when the lectures were delivered. The reader may notice a contrast in mood between my attempt to suggest the full darkness of what has already happened, together with the nature of the threat that hangs over the whole world, and my expression of the hope that the tide may yet be turned before the European tyranny is consolidated. Elsewhere I have expressed the conviction that America should give the most effective aid to the British people who are fighting to realize that hope. This conviction will be supported indirectly by my suggestions concerning what is at stake in the world in Chapter One and by my discussion of Christian pacifism in Chapter Four, but I have not sought to make this book a contribution to the current debate concerning American foreign policy.

The primary reference of the word "Realism" in the title is to the conviction pervading the book that Christianity avoids the illusions of both the optimists and the pessimists. I believe that the liberal optimism of the past generation and the theologians who deduce their view of human possibilities from a dogma of original sin which goes beyond the evidence are both wrong.

There is a secondary reference contained in the

word "Realism"—to the Realism of philosophical discussion. The lines between Realism and Idealism in contemporary thought are difficult to draw with precision. But there is a difference in emphasis between those who are most impressed by the *given* aspects of the world and those who are most impressed by the contribution of the mind to experience. Those who stress the given aspects of the world are less tempted to explain away anything that they find in the real that is not rational; they can believe more naturally that God is himself confronted by a limitation of given possibilities growing out of the temporal character of the world and out of the fact that history is moulded in part by finite wills which God himself does not coerce; they can more easily find a place for a revelation of God that is given to us in events rather than in the universal principles of reason. In this book I have not developed this side of Christian Realism though it is implied in what I say about the Christian faith and philosophy in Chapter One and about God's relation to evil in Chapter Two. Though I do not associate myself with the tirades against all Idealism that are now common in theology influenced by either Barth or Marx (*e.g.*, Brunner and Macmurray), it does seem to me to be true that the speculative systems of post-Kantian Idealism do represent that pride of autonomous reason against which there is such a strong reaction. But I see no pride in the kind of reason that never gets far away from the given elements in experience. Reason that is disciplined by facts and that leaves many questions open is less suggestive of pride than the faith that breeds dogmatism in theology.

Chapters Four and Five are the reworking of material that has been given in lectures delivered on the Earl Foundation at the Pacific School of Religion, on the Chancellor Foundation at Queens Theological College in Canada, on the Alden-Tuthill Foundation at the Chicago Theological Seminary. I am grateful to those institutions for their kindness and their encouragement and hope that other material given in connection with those lectureships will some day take the form of a book on the validity of the Christian Faith. This book does not deal directly with that problem. I have gone on the principle that in the end exposition is the best defense of Christianity.

I want to thank the editor of the *Journal of Religion* and its publisher, the University of Chicago Press, for permission to publish the appendix on "The Problem of Evil," which first appeared in the pages of its issue for October, 1938; and also the editor of *Religion in Life* and its publisher, the Abingdon-Cokesbury Press, for permission to use in Chapter Four selected material from an article entitled "The Christian's Ethical Decision" published in the summer number, 1940.

I am indebted to Mr. William L. Savage of Charles Scribner's Sons for invaluable editorial help.

J. C. B.

Pacific School of Religion,
Berkeley, California,
January, 1941.

CONTENTS

CHAPTER ONE

OUR NEW SITUATION

As a result of the events of the past year we know that we live in a new age, an age which we do not yet understand but which arouses in us deep foreboding. This chapter will be an attempt to outline some of the aspects of the new world situation which will have most influence upon Christian thinking and upon the life of the Church. There are many elements in the situation which are still unpredictable, but whatever events the next years may bring forth there are some characteristics of this new situation which will profoundly influence our lives. Those who speak about this new situation are usually classified as inhabitants of a dream world or as psychological victims of the war—so difficult is it to be or to seem objective in one's attitude to it. This new situation in which we live may be a better one in which to make Christianity seem true and relevant—at least in those parts of the world where there is still freedom to teach a relevant form of Christianity at all; but

Christianity will necessarily be taught with a different emphasis and to people who have lost faith in much that has been identified in their minds with the gospel.

The first of the underlying factors with which we must now reckon is the end of the spiritual unity of the Christian West, a unity based upon a combination of Christianity and humanism as the sources of the moral standards recognized by the conscience of the West.

We used to live in a world in which people generally realized that Christian standards had a claim upon them, in which minorities could speak freely and keep national life under judgment in the light of those standards, in which those who exercised power were at least inhibited by the scruples of their own or of other peoples' Christian conscience. Europe and America—the so-called West—belonged to that world, and we were conscious of membership in a common moral universe of discourse. It is the unity of that world that has been shattered and in most of its parts the authority of Christian standards is more seriously threatened than at any time since the days of Charlemagne. So long as we were able to take that kind of world for granted we thought little of it. Did we not find ourselves saying at times that good healthy paganism would be better than nominal Christianity? But we usually assumed that our healthy pagans would retain the Christian ethic. We now see that even watered-down Christianity had an important function in the community and that at least it preserved an environment within which a more prophetic Christianity could gain a hearing. We see now how many opportunities were thrown away in that world that did lip service to Christian standards, and we know what we have lost as we see a frankly pagan civilization take shape before our eyes.

Let me give one illustration that suggests how standards by which we do not live constantly affect our conduct. No one can say that in America we live according to a high standard of interracial justice, but we know in our hearts that every institution that perpetuates racial discrimination is wrong. We are on the defensive when we consent to such wrong. The accepted standards are a very important leverage for all who are seeking to realize interracial justice in our national life. Contrast that situation with what happens when racial discrimination is taught as a good, when anti-Semitism is an officially recognized policy, supported by the agencies that mould public opinion as a higher form of morality than interracial justice.

Until the signing of the Russian-German pact it appeared that the Christian-humanistic standards of the West would be supplanted by positive ideologies —especially Communism and National Socialism. But events that followed have in large part discredited those ideologies. Though the ideologies as consistent philosophies of life have themselves fallen on evil days, they had already done their negative work in undermining the Christian-humanistic standards over large areas. Moreover they still provide materials for the rationalizing of policies based upon disregard of objective truth and upon denial of the dignity of the individual or of the claims of all human groups. We now have the loss of the common ethos of the West with nothing to take its place save a struggle for power that is cloaked with nationalism and which takes the form of a revolutionary drive against the centers of respectability and privilege of the pre-war world of which the British Empire has become the chief symbol. The fact that this struggle for power and this revolutionary drive have been combined with extensive economic planning for a collective purpose makes them attractive to masses who have suffered because capitalistic institutions did not and seemingly could not solve the problem of unemployment.

There is a second major fact about this new age of ours which few of us have taken seriously as a possibility. We have to learn, what has been hidden from us by a combination of wishful idealism and natural incredulity, that nothing is too terrible to be possible. I refer to the extension of political tyranny by means of military victory over the whole continent of Europe. This development may be paralleled by a similar one in Asia. The combination of political tyranny and military victory is something new in the modern period and the instruments of control made possible by modern technology are new in human history. We had experience of military victory in 1918 and we soon learned to condemn the result, but even that victory did not expose the people of the defeated nations to the secret police of the victors. Even that victory did not destroy the cultural and religious freedom of the defeated nations nor did it, judging from the result, destroy the means of rapid recuperation. Political tyranny we knew and hated, but for the most part it was limited to those countries where at least a large section of the population desired its fruits and it was made more tolerable because it was united with symbols of national pride. But today we see military victory used to extend political tyranny over great nations that loathe it.

I hear many people say: "Do not become too excited for man has often suffered before and no crisis appears to have the same importance to history as to those who live through it." It is well to be so warned. But let us not forget that we have today vastly more effective means of centralized control, of suppressing revolts, of ferreting out opponents and eliminating places of refuge, of insulating a population against the truth and carrying official propaganda to every household, of taking children away from parental influence and moulding their souls to fit a pattern approved by those who exercise political power. The tyrant has at his back air-power as a final weapon that he can use as a threat at the first sign of resistance.

And let us remember this also: the modern tyrant has no fear of God or of Hell. It is a great mistake to suppose that present trends are a return to the Middle Ages. In the Middle Ages rulers were afraid of God or of Hell and they shared power with a Church which represented universal standards. As I have said, the modern tyrant does not even recognize as binding upon him the standards which have always been in the background of our civilization. What has been destroyed for the present on the European continent is not merely what we call "Democracy" but all government by law and all recognition that those who are governed have rights before the law and before God. What we have long called secularism has reached its limit for now God is not only denied in practice but He is also denied in theory and as a result the denial in practice becomes more complete.

We all know that this pattern cannot continue forever. It is impossible for pride and the lust for power to build towers of Babel that will endure. Death itself is a guarantee of change. To recognize this fact is to have the beginning of hope, but our generation may not see a better order in Europe if Germany is allowed to consolidate her power. Even if the continental tyranny should be destroyed after a decade, it might then be followed by new wars, especially civil wars. If the tyranny lasts long enough to destroy the roots of the institutions which make possible peaceful change within nations, if all the habits of free public opinion are abandoned, then those who seek escape from this situation have no recourse save conspiracy and revolt. Moreover, these next years will give the worst native elements in each of the defeated nations a chance to enjoy power. Native fascists, traitors, spies, informers, carpetbaggers, those who are not sensitive about the role of local agent of foreign tyranny will have their day. There may be enough of these and their followers to turn revolt into civil war. I say these hard things because it is important that we not deceive ourselves with false hopes based upon the thought that tyranny supported by violence and terror cannot last. It is true that it cannot last but it can destroy the conditions on which peaceful changes depend and its end in our time may be bloody chaos.

We can take hope from the certainty that this chaos will pass also.[1]

When I say these things, my purpose is not to make moral judgments upon any nation. When we enter that region of moral judgment we find that the guilt for these developments is shared by all of us. It was the Western democracies, including ourselves, which were the masters of the world until a few years ago and it was in large part their failure to cooperate with rational elements in Germany and their vain attempt to preserve an indefensible *status quo* that caused the present madness. We in the Christian West have been punished because we tried to ride two horses at the same time. We tried to maintain a respect for Christian and humanistic standards and we complacently enjoyed the privileges of imperialism. If we had been more Christian we might have been spared this punishment. If we had been more imperialistic the punishment might have been postponed, although it would have come in the end.

I do not suggest that the majority of the people of

[1]We cannot see far into the future but there are grounds for hope that the tide will be turned sooner than seemed likely when the lectures on which this book is based were delivered. The British have preserved a foothold for freedom in Europe and have reduced the threat of the Axis to the rest of the world. We can thank the people of Britain for the hope that we now have that Germany may be unable to consolidate her power. The realization of that hope depends now upon America as much as upon Britain, upon America's organization of her national life in order to give Britain the most needed aid. It is still far from easy to see by what steps the nations on the continent can be freed. The danger of a long period of anarchy and civil wars in parts of Europe will remain even if Hitler is defeated.

any nation have been perverted in mind and soul by what has happened. The forces that have made possible this extension of political tyranny through military victory have been able to take advantage of high as well as low elements in human nature, for they have channelled into destructive and anti-social channels the loyalty and devotion of countless persons, especially youth. When we come to assess blame and when we come to consider the personal qualities of the rank and file of the people in all nations involved in this common tragedy, including our own, the picture is a very complex one. But that fact does not cancel the objective situation that has been created by the possession of new forms of power by those who have the will to use them without restraint in the consolidating of a continental tyranny.

I have sketched what appear to be two factors in this new age of ours—the break-up of the moral unity of the West and the successful use of military victory to extend the area of political tyranny.

What can we expect as some of the spiritual consequences of this new situation? I shall mention three such consequences which will be of special importance for the preaching of the gospel and for the life of the Christian Church everywhere.

1. Hopelessness.

The first of these consequences is that we shall find on all sides great hopelessness. Even before the Second World War began to show its character, this hopelessness was present among the younger generation wherever it was not drugged by nationalism. In a survey of the attitudes of European students at the beginning of the Second World War, it was found that the most common attitude was one of cynicism combined with a strange inertia, a paralysis of effort. Today we shall find people in conquered countries even more hopeless as they think of their own future and as they look at their children. This will be true of the most sensitive people in every country. In Germany and Italy, there will be this feeling among the minorities which have opposed National Socialism or Fascism. The bitterness of being unable even to speak about this fate or to organize in the open for common action will increase the hopelessness. There will be for many of the finest spirits a terrible moral conflict arising from the fact that they must choose between silence, which will be taken for acquiescence in the face of oppression and official lies, and martyrdom which will be costly to their families. Martyrdom may never be futile but under these efficient tyrannies it can be so covered up or so misrepresented by those who control the channels of information that it must often seem futile to those whom it confronts.

This feeling of hopelessness of which I speak will be all the more acute because it comes in a period in which we have known such high hopes. Our generation has been relatively idealistic and sensitive in its moral judgments. The much-discussed cynicism of youth is in part the reverse side of moral sensitivity. Between the two World Wars ours has been to an extraordinary extent a pacifist generation. We can remember the Wilsonian era, the founding of the League of Nations, Locarno, the long vain struggle for disarmament, the Kellogg Pact, the crusades of absolute pacifists meeting with a wide response. We know what is happening to us and we know what has been lost. There have been days of as great external calamity before. But I doubt if there have been days when men on such a large scale have been so conscious of a rapid descent from hope to hopelessness. When the world went through the agony of the First World War it was sustained by the faith that the war would be the beginning of a better world. Today many have had to endure war without that faith and to face the future without freedom and without being able to see any choice ahead save the choice at some future time between tyranny and civil war. This seems almost too much for the human spirit.

One of the most buoyant of the younger Christian leaders, after a period of four weeks in occupied France, writes of his impressions: "I found it intolerably hard not to lose heart as I prayed for a lost Europe and a lost world. I suppose I have been slow in coming to the edge of the abyss, but those weeks in France brought me there. The sheer human misery of the refugees, the fickleness of international alliances, the chilly menace of material power on the souls of men—all showed how far we have gone, apart from all chances of victory or defeat, in the way that leadeth to destruction. And so to think about the future became a mental torture."

A second consequence of this new situation which will be of great spiritual importance is that we shall have difficulty in dealing with the fact that it has been force that has so quickly changed the face of the world. It is sobering to realize how much has been effected by superiority in tanks and bombing planes. An English theologian, V. A. Demant, wrote in 1934: "Where everything in the secular world seems to conspire against belief in the supremacy of the Spirit, the task of upholding faith in divine Providence will become more and more difficult for the Christian Church."[2]

Those words were written under the influence of the economic depression in view of the extent to which impersonal forces seemed to cramp personal life. How much more obvious truth there is in those words now than there was in 1934! Is not God on the side of the heaviest battalions after all? We know that He is not but how much harder it will be for people to believe it. Will it not seem to Americans engaged in feverish military preparations quite as much as to people in Europe and Asia that there is a military determination of history which is primary? What can the spirit of man do when men are silenced by overwhelming force, when there is no sounding board of free opinion, when there is efficient undermining, through teaching, censorship, propaganda and terror, of those standards a common acceptance of which is presupposed in all moral influence, in all work of the spirit? How can the God of love work in a world made over by those who have the most efficient weapons? That tormenting question must be the burden of much Christian thinking, preaching, and praying.

There is one other consequence which will profoundly affect the life of the Christian Church. For a time on the continent of Europe, except in Switzerland, there will not be one Church that is free to speak about this world. The Church will not be destroyed.

[2]V. A. Demant, *God, Man and Society,* page 23.

Men will still be able to worship and to speak about God and His relation to the individual soul. The sacraments of the Catholic Churches will still be available to the faithful in many nations. Catholicism has an advantage because after it has compromised beyond the limit that seems tolerable to most Protestants it still has the sacraments and therefore, from its perspective, it can afford to wait. The Bible still will be circulated and read. Perhaps it will be read more than usual. In that fact may lie hope of new beginnings, for the Bible will keep alive knowledge of God and of moral standards and it will be the chief bond of union between Christians in a broken world. Once again the Bible may become the source of men's vision of liberty.

One European leader has suggested that the Churches in this new Europe will be "Churches without space." They will be unable to deal directly with the problems of this world. The emphasis will be upon pietism, apocalyptic and other-worldly hopes, and traditionalism. The Church will undergo the same inner conflict that will torture the most sensitive individuals. How far should it compromise with the new order to preserve its own existence? The relations between Churches on the continent and the Anglo-Saxon Churches will become more difficult to maintain but they will be of even greater importance than they have ever been. In many of the countries under foreign domination the Church may become even more influential than it is now for it will represent not only Christianity but lost national freedom. In indirect ways the Church, forced to be silent about this world, may speak about freedom. The Church in Europe, partly underground, partly compromised, partly silenced, still will be a witness to the truth about God and man upon which alone the Europe beyond this tragic new Europe of the dictators can be built.

It will be in a peculiar way the responsibility of the American Churches first to understand the Churches that have lost freedom, and thus avoid self-righteousness when Churches under great pressure seem to compromise; second, to help them to preserve their institutions and to carry out their work under handicaps; and, third, to supplement them by keeping alive forms of Christian witness that are impossible for them. We are not fit for this responsibility, but in all the uncertainties of this age, amidst all the differences of opinion among us, here at least is clear guidance. God is calling American Christians to live through their Churches for the Church everywhere.

These consequences are both present realities and threats hanging over an indefinite future. These threats may be banished by the defeat of Hitler if that is followed by wise statesmanship that will not only release conquered countries from external oppression but also prepare the way for a "New Order" based upon consent. It is difficult to chart such a course now and past experience does not give ground for confidence that a long and terrible war will leave enough wisdom and magnanimity in places of power to bring about that result. Yet, after such chastisement, there may come again in our time a moment of free choice in which a better possibility will confront humanity than is now the case. For that moment we can live today.

The First World War and its aftermath resulted in

a revolution in Christian thinking in Europe. Karl Barth was the great disturber who shattered the complacency of modernist, or liberal, Christianity and who asked the questions with which the Christian mind has struggled for the past twenty years. I shall not attempt here to describe the theological ferment of those years. In many ways that seem strange to most Americans, Christians who have been influenced by the Barthian impulse in theology have been saying to the Church: "Thou shalt have no other gods before me" . . . and "ye must be born again." They have attacked the tendency to set up human philosophies, human ideals, human causes, human institutions—especially the state, and even the Church—in place of God.

Their attack upon modern Christianity has been essentially the same as that which recently has come from quite a different quarter, the editors of *Fortune,* who have said that when men listen to the Church they hear what they themselves have said—when their great need is to hear "the sound of a voice, not our voice, but a voice coming from something not ourselves, in the existence of which we cannot disbelieve."[3] It is a striking fact that the strange, strident voice of Karl Barth, speaking in language that is so traditional and appearing to us to be so obscurantist, and these young and sophisticated American laymen should raise essentially the same question. Also this new theological movement has called us to recognize that man needs a far more radical change than has been contemplated by modern Christianity, that the classical

[3]*Fortune,* January, 1940 (Reprinted in *The Christian Century,* January 3, 1940).

Christian conception of man's sin still points to the deepest level of the human problem. "Thou shalt have no other gods before me." "Ye must be born again."

There has been some attempt to discount this change of thought in Europe on the ground that, as one writer has put it, it is the result of a peculiarly European psychosis.[4] But that view of the matter fails to recognize how far it is true that men who are facing the tragedies of life, who are reminded of their own sin and limitations, may see aspects of the truth that are hid from the complacent and the self-sufficient. In fact they may see permanent human problems in bold relief. Every one of us is rendered one-sided in thinking and in religious insight to some degree by accidental circumstance. This means that we must listen to those who in different historical situations have been prepared to understand aspects of the Christian message that have never spoken to our condition.

The Second World War and its aftermath are likely to have a profound influence upon American religious thought and life. But I do not believe that we shall experience here a mere repetition of what has happened for the past two decades in Europe. For one thing we have already become so familiar with the European development that no Karl Barth can arise here and say the same things to us as a new challenge. Our own thinkers have been changing their minds for a decade, in part under the influence of the Barthian impulse in theology. Moreover, we have the advantage of the years of criticism of Barthian theology. Brun-

[4]E. E. Aubrey in *Christendom,* Spring, 1938.

ner's criticism of Barth leads to a far less intransigent and less one-sided theology. John Baillie's criticisms of both Barth and Brunner are perhaps the best example of the attempt of Anglo-Saxon thinkers to face the questions raised by Barth and push through to different answers.[5] The fact that Barth has been forced to change his own mind as the result of recent events in such a way as to modify his conception of the gulf between all human ideals and institutions and the will of God is also important in preventing us from becoming blind followers of Barth in the next period. For years Barth taught that all political institutions were so completely controlled by sin that the Christian as a Christian could not identify himself with any one of them. But it finally dawned upon him that National Socialism was so black that democracy was at least gray in comparison. In his latest writings he has been calling for the defense of democracy as a Christian task.[6]

Another reason for believing that American Christianity, though it will be profoundly influenced by the tragic and frustrating character of the Second World War, will not merely repeat what European Christianity has already gone through is that we are not tempted to absolutize the theology of the Reformation. I have no doubt that we shall come to have a more Bible-centered type of Christianity but I am quite sure that we shall not read the Bible under the guidance of sixteenth-century confessions of faith. Nor are we likely

[5]John Baillie, *Our Knowledge of God,* Chapter I.
[6]See especially: Karl Barth, *The Church and the Political Problem of Our Day.*

to develop an attitude of piety toward the texts of Luther and Calvin. Concentration upon a particular period in the past as the golden age of theology is alien to our habits of thinking.[7]

There is also among us what I can only call an empirical temper that even the present catastrophes are not likely to destroy. We are distrustful of ambitious theological schemes based upon dogmas that are never fully criticized in the light of what they mean in terms of concrete experience. We have a sceptical attitude toward sweeping statements about human depravity, or about the status of non-Christian religions, or about the authority of revelation. We desire to know more clearly what a doctrine of sin means psychologically or in terms of actual social experience, and when we hear about such ideas as the doctrine of the two natures of Christ or the theory of the impersonal humanity of Christ we press for some explanation of what those ideas mean for our understanding of Jesus Christ as a concrete human individual. When we hear pious words about the Church, with a capital C, we desire to know how those words apply to the very familiar and very human institutions in our communities which we call churches. This empirical temper seems to me to be a quite necessary corrective for traditional ways of thinking and I see few signs of even a

[7]In Emil Brunner's *The Philosophy of Religion* we have a frank avowal of this concentration. The author writes: "As starting point, as the pattern of a Christian knowledge of revelation, we may choose the Reformation confession of faith as being that expression of faith which, although outside the Bible, most clearly expresses the view that the faith founded on the Scriptures takes of itself." Page 22.

temptation to abandon it.[8] For these reasons we can expect to see the development of a type of thought in this country that is no mere copy of what we read in European theological books but which will be oriented toward many of the problems that have occupied the attention of European thinkers.

Though we need not follow blindly the thinkers of continental Europe, we must not reject their contribution blindly either. They have been wiser than we concerning the depths of sin and tragedy in human life. They have been wiser than we in seeing that we cannot make an easy transition from the assumptions of the modern university and of modern culture generally to the Christian faith. They have been wiser than we in insisting that we can only discover Christian truth when our minds are formed by response to the Bible and to the Christian tradition, and if our minds, our canons of judgment, are formed by nationalism or by popular brands of naturalism we can only find Christianity intellectually credible if we have a conversion at the level of our deepest assumptions. They have been wrong when they have suggested that there is complete discontinuity between reason and faith,

[8]Reinhold Niebuhr, who would often be classified among those who have deserted this empirical way of thinking, says of an idea in theology that he is seeking to refute: "There are no historical realities which remotely conform to it. It is important to recognize this lack of conformity to the facts of experience as a form of heresy. All forms of religious faith are principles of interpretation which we use to organize our experience." One could hardly have a better statement of what I am referring to as the empirical temper that pervades American thought and which is not limited to schools of thought which claim the name "Empiricism." (See *Christianity and Power Politics,* page 6.)

between Christianity and the higher insights of the race known apart from Christian influence. They have been wrong when they have said that we cannot find confirmations of Christian truth in the results of science, in the observation of events or in the conscience of man.

In the next chapter I shall attempt to give content to these statements by outlining the Christian conception of God and its meaning for us. No amount of speculative philosophy could have given us that conception of God. It came to naïve minds as they reflected upon events. But when once we see the conception of God as it is given to us in the Bible, we find that it throws light on many intellectual problems, that it is extraordinarily relevant to our social strivings, that it meets the needs of the inner life, that it gives what seems to be a necessary background to those moral demands which we cannot disobey without a sense of guilt, that it can enter not into one but into many philosophical systems, finally breaking through all of them and yet still holding the minds of men so that they seek once again to make it the center of a philosophy. We have seen this happen in the case of Platonism, Aristotelianism, Cartesian rationalism, Romanticism, Kantianism, Hegelianism, Personalism, various forms of Realism, and now we even have a few Christian Marxists and Christian naturalists. These are all precarious alliances, some of them more precarious than others, but that all of them have been thought possible is striking evidence of the universality and adequacy of the Christian conception of God.

Most liberal Christians in America have taken for

granted an alliance between Christianity and one or another of the more recent of these philosophies. I believe that the time has come for us to give less attention to the philosophical partner in the alliance and more attention to the Biblical and Christian element in it. That is the most clearly valid point in the theology of Barth. As one attempts to do this, one should seek also to avoid the substitution of credulity for the critical temper that is the most clearly valid element in Liberalism. As I observe our contemporaries who go back to the Bible or to tradition, it seems to me that they quickly become credulous and come to believe too easily what they find in the tradition. They fill the gaps in their thought too cheaply with doctrines that have been formulated in another period. It is important for us to orient ourselves toward the tradition, to explore the Bible more than has been our custom. We should take seriously the insight of such men as Paul and Augustine and Aquinas and Luther, but we must continue to test all that we find in the light of the persistent facts of our experience.

CHAPTER TWO

GOD AND HIS ACTIVITY

TO SPEAK about God with any degree of adequacy one must be a poet or prophet or mystic. The prose of the theologian when he speaks of God is abstract and forbidding, but such prose is all that I can command. All our words are derived from experiences that are less than the experience of God for God is utterly unique and incomparable. Some mystics prefer negations when they speak of God but negations are as misleading as faltering attempts to say positively what God is and what God does.

Within that stream of life and reflection which we call the Hebrew-Christian tradition there has been wrought out over a period of more than a thousand years a conception of God and His activity which commands both our minds and our hearts. This conception of God is no product of the academic mind, for men came to it as they struggled with the problems of personal and social life, as they faced pain and death and national collapse. It is the product of work and suffering and prayer together with reflection upon those experiences. It was tested by a cross and it was confirmed by that triumph over defeat and death that we call the resurrection. Philosophers and theologians did not first develop this conception of God but when it had been given to them they made it the center of many a system of philosophy and theology.

This chapter will consist of four affirmations about God and His activity which are involved in the conception of God that meets us in the Bible and to which many of us find ourselves returning after vain attempts to develop substitutes for it to please the fancy of modern man.

These four great affirmations about God gain their significance largely from the fact that all four belong together. Take any one of them and emphasize it to the exclusion of the others and we do not have the Christian conception of God at all. The four affirmations are these: (1) God is the creator. (2) God is the God of righteousness. (3) God is the Lord of history. (4) God is the redeemer. As I discuss each of these Christian convictions about God, keep in mind all of the others, for it is the combination of cosmic power and righteousness and mercy in the God who is the Lord of history that gives to the Christian faith in God its distinctiveness and adequacy.

1. *God is the creator.* To say this is not to suggest that we have light on the mysteries of creation. When the theologians insisted that God created the world out of nothing, they did not seek to explain the source of the materials of creation but rather to affirm the absolute dependence of the world on God. When we

say that God is the creator we mean that the object of our supreme devotion is one with the reality upon which we depend for existence. We mean that man depends upon God and not God upon the desires and imagination of men. We mean that the word "God" is not merely another and more pious name for the process of nature and history which we observe but that the process of nature and history points beyond itself to God on whom it depends.

A false issue has been raised at this point by Professor John Dewey. He continually insists that if God is the transcendent being on whom the process of nature and history depends, then we need not seek to realize ideals in history but instead need only to contemplate their realization as already complete in God. Christian theism seems to him, therefore, to undercut the human attempt to embody values in experience. But he fails to distinguish between the Greek idea of God as a self-sufficient being whose end is to contemplate Himself and the Hebrew idea of God as a worker—to use John Macmurray's word. God does not depend upon the process of nature and history for His existence but God does have purposes that can only be realized in nature and history, purposes which are not realized now, purposes that cannot be realized if men continue to resist God. Human instruments are necessary for God's activity in human life. To say that God is the creator is quite different from saying that God is the self-sufficient absolute.[1]

[1] John Dewey, *A Common Faith,* pages 45–46.

This is a theme which pervades all of Dewey's discussions of religion and of classical philosophy. Charles Hartshorne comments on this emphasis of Dewey's: "The error is the

To say that God is the creator is to say that God is power as well as goodness. It is to say that value and reality belong together. It is to say that God can be trusted in spite of the appearances of evil and defeat in this world, for this world is not our world and it is not the dictators' world but it is God's world. When we can say nothing else in moments of bafflement, when we are tempted to despair, we can say that. The prophet of the exile, Second Isaiah, at the time of national collapse, gained courage and hope from the faith that God was cosmic power—capable of bringing redemption to his people in spite of their helplessness as exiles, a kind of helplessness that has become too familiar to our generation. It gave the prophet support to know that "the nations are as a drop of a bucket, and are counted as the small dust of the balance: behold, he taketh up the isles as a very little

---

idea of a being in all respects perfect, hence unchangeable, unenrichable, indifferent (impassive) to all loss or gain or results of striving. The alternative is, it is as clear as arithmetic, not the denial that there is a being truly perfect, but only the denial that there is a being *in all respects* perfect. For a being in some respects (say in knowledge) perfect, but in some respects capable of increase in value (say in satisfaction, happiness) would not in the least imply the irrelevance of human striving or of change. Human achievements in knowledge might then not indeed increase the accuracy of God's knowledge of the real, but by adding new content, new objects, for him to know accurately (for our knowledge itself would be known by him) might increase the variety, richness, beauty of the divine experience and so the divine happiness. Thus God could literally be 'served' " (*The Christian Century,* March 6, 1940).

The idea of God that Prof. Hartshorne points to in this passage is consistent with the Christian conception of God. Against that Dewey's criticisms are irrelevant.

thing." . . . "Have ye not known? have ye not heard? hath it not been told you from the beginning? have ye not understood from the foundations of the earth? It is he that sitteth upon the circle of the earth, and the inhabitants thereof are as grasshoppers; that stretcheth out the heavens as a curtain and spreadeth them out as a tent to dwell in: that bringeth princes to nothing; he maketh the judges of the earth as vanity" (Isaiah 40:15; 40:21–23). To say such things as that may, of course, lead to fatalism, but when this perception of God's cosmic power is combined with faith in His righteousness and in His redeeming love such words are the final ground for hope that the world will not be forever subjected to those who at the moment exercise the most power within it.

To say that God is the creator is also to say that He is universal. All races and nations are His creatures. It is interesting that in the book of Amos, the first of the Old Testament prophets to see clearly the universality of God, there are passages about God's control of the cosmos which according to most scholars have been added at a later time because they fitted the central insight of the book. It is not enough for Amos to say: "Are ye not as children of the Ethiopians unto me, O children of Israel? saith the Lord. Have not I brought up Israel out of the land of Egypt? and the Philistines from Caphtor, and the Syrians from Kir?" Beside those great sentences a later editor has put these words: "It is he that buildeth his chambers in the heavens, and hath founded his vault upon the earth; he that calleth for the waters of the sea and poureth them out upon the face of the earth: the

Lord is his name."[2] It is no accident that those two passages are found together for it is obvious that the creator of the world is no provincial deity.

Emphasis upon God as the creator is the surest way of protecting ourselves from idolatry. It underlines the uniqueness of God, God's independence of everything human. In His being God transcends man because He is the creator. Many theologians seize upon this idea of creation and carry it a step further which seems to me to be without warrant. It is often assumed that there is an absolute contrast between the creator and all His creatures. For example, Professor Brunner writes that "the greatest dissimilarity between two things which we can express at all—more dissimilar than light and darkness, death and life, good and evil, is that between the creator and that which is created."[3] As is often the case with Brunner, on the next page he qualifies this contrast by saying that the fact that man is a creature "binds man fast to God" for God is present "operatively" in His creation.

Brunner's emphasis upon the absolute contrast between God and His creatures is one aspect of the idea of the complete transcendence of God that is emphasized by the Dialectical Theology. But we should separate in our thinking two kinds of transcendence. There is the transcendence in being or existence which

[2]Amos 9:6–7. The words in which Israel is put on the same level as the other nations are a good example of what is meant by revelation. Here is a word that comes to us out of events. It is stated with a minimum of abstractness. It was so novel that one marvels that it could have been said, but when once it is said it is permanent.

[3]*Man in Revolt,* page 90.

clearly goes with the idea of God as creator. If the known world were to be wiped out God would still be God. There is also the transcendence of complete otherness or unlikeness that need not follow at all from the idea of God as creator. In his dependence upon God man is unlike God, but that does not imply total unlikeness. In fact that only follows when it is maintained by a doctrinaire theology that sin wholly destroys the image of the creator which, according to Christian teaching, was imparted to man as the creature. In the next chapter more will be said about this point. My concern here is to suggest that it does not necessarily follow from the metaphysical gulf between the creator and those dependent upon Him for existence that the creator is wholly unlike His creatures.

2. *God is the God of righteousness.* This is the second great affirmation about God. To speak of the righteousness of God is to point to that which judges every human moral achievement and every human moral standard, but it is a great error to suggest that the righteousness of God is totally other than what we human beings recognize as righteousness. One of the common refrains of contemporary theology, especially under Lutheran influence, is an attack upon moralism. Reinhold Niebuhr who represents this on one side of his thought says that the way in which to curb human pretensions is to emphasize the conviction "that there is a transcendent perspective from which 'all our righteousnesses are as filthy rags.' Implied in such a faith is the sense of a goodness which not only fulfills, but may negate, the highest human goodness. This is the implication developed in the Book of Job, when

God refuses to be judged by human standards of justice and quiets the protests of Job by overawing him with the mysteries of the world beyond human ken."[4] The truth in this position is that there are times in which we must question even our highest moral ideals because there are so many subtle ways in which we confuse our ideals with cultural habits, interests, prejudices. But when this is done it should be done for the sake of recovering in purer form the highest human perceptions of goodness rather than to revert to the worship of blank transcendence, much less, cosmic power. The righteousness of God as we know it in the Bible, righteousness which does not negate the highest human aspirations toward goodness but rather those corruptions of goodness to which the "good man" is most tempted, is sufficient to keep all human pretensions and all human interests under judgment. Paul in his classical statement of what it means to feel a sense of sin does not trace his feeling to a view of God's demands which transcend human morality but to confrontation by an intelligible human moral standard: "Thou shalt not covet" (Romans 7:7).

There are times when we should dwell upon such words as these: "For my thoughts are not your thoughts, neither are your ways my ways, saith the Lord. For as the heavens are higher than the earth, so are my ways higher than your ways, and my thoughts than your thoughts" (Isaiah 55:8,9). But we must come back constantly to the question: "Shall not the judge of all the earth do right?" (Genesis 18:25). To preserve human moral distinctions but to

[4] *An Interpretation of Christian Ethics,* page 230.

know that no one of us is without sin, to exalt the highest standards of goodness that we know but to realize how prone we are to use those highest standards to sanction our own desires—that is the difficult way which we should take.

The righteousness of God that we find in the Bible receives its content from ideas concerning human relations which negate most human practice but fulfill our highest human aspirations after goodness. The prophets saw the righteousness of God in terms of human justice, often in terms of economic justice. "For three transgressions of Israel, yea, for four, I will not turn away the punishment thereof; because they have sold the righteous for silver and the needy for a pair of shoes" (Amos 2:6). This emphasis upon the moral test of right relations with God as the God of righteousness is something that all of us take for granted, but it is easy to forget what a great inheritance it is. It has not usually been taken for granted by religion. Even the Jewish religion has often buried it under a mass of ceremonial laws and Christians must constantly rediscover it. It is endangered when we allow our stress upon God's transcendence of all human morality to be more than a means of purging away our misuse of the highest human moral insights. The Christian faith that God is known to us supremely in Christ, unless it is accompanied by the rejection of the revelation through the concrete personality of Christ, guarantees the continuity between God's righteousness and the highest human goodness. Men are more likely to be humbled in their pretensions in a significant way as they face the embodiment of divine goodness in Christ than when, as in the case of Job, they face the power and the majesty of God in the cosmos.

Three sentences from three different traditions in the New Testament, one from the Sermon on the Mount, one from the First Epistle of John, and the third from Paul, indicate how central the moral test of right relations with God are in Christianity: "If therefore thou art offering thy gift before the altar, and there rememberest that thy brother hath aught against thee, leave there thy gift before the altar, and go thy way, first be reconciled to thy brother, and then come and offer thy gift" (Matthew 5:23–24). "If any man say, I love God, and hateth his brother, he is a liar: for he that loveth not his brother whom he hath seen, cannot love God whom he hath not seen" (1 John 4:20–21). "But now abideth faith, hope, love, these three; and the greatest of these is love" (1 Cor. 13:13). It is well to be reminded in these days that the ethical emphasis in the New Testament is not limited to the Sermon on the Mount.

3. *God is the Lord of history.* This third affirmation about God follows naturally from the second. Christians rather recently have come to see how important this affirmation is and how far it represents a distinctive Christian position. By history I mean the irreversible sequence of events which occur in time and which are the stuff of our human experience. These events belong both to our private and to our public life but it is the events belonging to our public life that are most remembered and which constitute the major part of what we think of as history. For

mystical and pantheistic religions, history has secondary importance but for the Jewish-Christian tradition history is the arena of God's activity that is most meaningful for human beings. What happens in history makes a difference to God Himself. As I have said, God is no self-sufficient absolute whose realm is an eternity that is above the world of time and change, of struggle and suffering. He has a will for men in this world, for their public life as well as for their private lives. This will is partly frustrated because men in their weakness and blindness and sin resist and disobey Him. Without this freedom to resist God the development of moral persons would be impossible. We see in the fact of this freedom not the explanation of all evil but the explanation of the greater part of the social evil that haunts us. God does not coerce us into obedience. He seeks to persuade us and He shares our struggles and has compassion on us for the sufferings which we bring upon ourselves.

It seems to be a fact that the social evil which pervades a whole civilization destroys faith and all sense of the meaningfulness of life more readily than such forms of natural evil as disease or earthquakes. The latter are borne by people in such a way that faith is often deepened. The impact of natural evil is limited because each soul or each relatively small group bears its own burden. And, as Sorley suggests, "each knows, also, better than any other can, what he is able to suffer and to do, and in the darkest hour he may descry a promise of dawn unseen by the onlooker."[5]

[5]W. R. Sorley, *Moral Values and the Idea of God,* page 345.

But in the case of war or the collapse of civilization a whole generation faces the same tragedy in such a way that for all the entire universe is darkened. In moments of actual crisis, so long as positive action is possible, there is a solidarity in suffering that makes the burden lighter but when crisis turns into a dull hopelessness with liberty gone and with no line of action open, we can expect the problem of evil to be present in its most acute form. And yet it is true that from the theological point of view this kind of social evil is more easily explained than the work of one disease germ. When once we admit the fact of human freedom to resist God as a necessary condition for the development of persons we can see how this moral recalcitrance on the part of man leads to the collapse of a civilization. Even from our human perspective we can see why it is that God cannot create an interdependent community of persons which is the basis of all love and fellowship without having at the same time a world in which evils spread and in which our sins and failures have incalculable consequences for the innocent.[6]

There is a tendency at present in Europe to return to the idea that there are superhuman forces of evil, fallen angels or devils, which prey upon human life and greatly extend the power of evil in the world. If such superhuman evil spirits do exist, their sin can be explained as the result of their freedom which they share with us. The only question is whether or not such beings exist. I believe that the present plight of

[6]For a more thorough discussion of the problem of evil in general see the Appendix.

humanity can be explained without resort to them as an explanation. If we put together the following factors which we know to be present in our experience we have explanation enough: human egoism, which is a universal fact, the limitations of our imagination and intelligence, the rapid development of complex problems with which our minds have not been prepared to deal, the cumulative character of the evil of the past leading to vicious circles of defeat and revenge, of hatred and fear, the powers of the few for controlling and blinding the many and the effect of the mere possession of those powers in creating a kind of madness in the souls of those who hold them, the amazing capacity of the human mind to make a partial interest seem a universal good, the way in which the devotion and courage of common folk can be turned by nationalism into hatred and cruelty, the new weapons of war which increase the destructiveness of impulses as old as the race. These evil-producing factors and many more exist in our experience. We can see how taken together they play havoc with our society. If we ascribe our plight to superhuman devils, we shall either neglect our real enemies or yield to the spirit of fatalism.[7]

After all allowance has been made for the factors which cause the social evil that makes it difficult for many of our contemporaries to believe in God as the Lord of history, we must now ask: how does God work in the events of our time?

How could God conceivably act—the God of the cos-

[7]I have elaborated this discussion of the causes of social evil in my chapter in *The Christian Faith and the Common Life,* by Nils Ehrenström and others.

mos—without swamping all finite creatures? It is entirely obvious that God does not act by writing His will across the sky so that all men can read and tremble. It is entirely obvious that God does not intervene between our deeds and their consequences so that men fail to reap what they sow even when the harvest is red with the blood of the innocent. In fact we do not observe that God even intervenes with an occasional miracle as He was believed to do in the days of the Bible. It would not tempt a responsible religious commentator on events to attribute the calm sea and the fog on the English Channel that facilitated the evacuation of Dunkirk to a divine miracle as the plague that defeated the hosts of Sennacherib before the gates of Jerusalem was interpreted as a miracle. No, the supernaturalism of direct intervention between our deeds and their consequences must be rejected. There is an order of consequences in nature and in the world of human events which God seems to respect and the pattern of which man must learn if he is to escape destruction. If it were otherwise we should have to believe that we live in a world of caprice in which God intervenes in behalf of His favorites only and that in the choice of His favorites there is no reason or justice. If He intervenes occasionally we cannot but cry out and ask why He does not intervene regularly. And we know that He does not intervene regularly.

Professor John Macmurray in his *The Clue to History* has effectively stated one way in which God acts in history. He says that Christianity is not to be associated with an ideal but with a description of the real world. There is revealed in Christ the nature of the divine intention for men and, although men may resist that intention, to do so is to go against the structure of life. He says this: "When men set out to realize an intention which is contrary to the divine intention, they do not achieve it. They achieve something that they did not intend. If the intention is the opposite of the divine intention, they then necessarily achieve, not what they intended, but its opposite."[8] I believe that Macmurray oversimplifies the problem and provides a too optimistic version of the way in which the divine intention corrects human behavior. He is right in calling attention to the fact that valid moral ideals are descriptions of the demands of reality. He is right in saying that men cannot realize for long that which is opposed to the divine intention. I am not sure that he is right in saying that, against their wills, men always realize the divine intention. He gives too little scope to human freedom to resist God and he does not see the full tragedy of life. What seems to be true is that while men may not for long realize an intention that is against the will of God, they may flounder around in the midst of a divine judgment without realizing in a positive way the intention of God. How long will they so flounder? We cannot say, but it would be impossible to set any definite limits to this human failure.

If we apply this principle to the immediate situation, we may say that it is certain that as long as those who exercise power in Europe, or anywhere else, seek to use the people of conquered nations as tools of a dominant race they will surely fail. There are limits to human endurance and sooner or later ex-

[8]Page 95.

ploited groups will find ways to curb or overthrow their exploiters. Economic production calls for incentives that slaves do not possess. I like to go back in these days to some words that antedate modern democracy and liberalism by nearly three thousand years and which in their context show that there are and always have been limits to men's endurance of tyranny. "Thy father made our yoke grievous: now therefore make thou the grievous service of thy father, and his heavy yoke which he put upon us, lighter, and we will serve thee" (1 Kings 12:4). Those words were the beginning of a revolution under a religious sanction. The failure to organize Europe or perhaps a larger part of the world on the basis of exploitation and injustice would not necessarily guarantee a stable order of justice. It might mean years of civil war and anarchy punctuated by new attempts at tyranny which in turn would fail. We cannot organize our common life permanently on a basis that is opposed to the intention of God but we can be so weak and blind and sinful that we fail to organize it in accordance with God's intention. Judgment and punishment may be all that lie ahead of us if it is only by this method that God works in history.

But there is another method. It is God's persuasion of men. One finds a great many forms of this persuasion. The mere threat of punishment is one form of it. The fact that men find that, if they persist in a way of life that runs against the divine intention, they bring upon themselves intolerable evil seems to be a necessary element in God's persuasion of men. Berdyaev[9] says that war is making itself impossible because

[9] *The Destiny of Man,* page 257.

of the development of the technique of war. Men will be driven to find ways to avoid war, for they know that it menaces even that for which they fight. There is also the constant influence of truth on the minds and consciences of men. The manipulation of the facts by official propaganda and the moulding of the souls of the rising generation to be responsive to an official philosophy of life are obstacles to the persuasive activity of God. But there are limits to this kind of perversion. It is incredible that men will be content to renounce for long freedom of expression. Official propaganda and official doctrines will often become self-contradictory, as they have been in the case of the official Nazi attitude toward Bolshelvism within a few years. *Lies have a way of cancelling each other in the end.* The promises of an authoritarian state to its people will have to be kept more faithfully than promises to other states. When in place of fulfilled promises there comes national disaster, disillusionment will take the place of credulity and minds may be opened to objective truth once more. Those who work only for narrow interests and who know that the word of each is worthless except as it is on the side of his interests cannot cooperate for long. There must be some honor among thieves if they are going to cooperate successfully, even when the thieves are nations.

God also persuades us through individuals who are controlled by faith and love, through minorities and remnants. There is a cumulative power in the work of those who have become in a peculiar way God's instruments of persuasion that is extraordinary. So pervasive is this tendency that every illustration of it appears to be trite. That very triteness is a testimony to the power of the persons and minorities that we all have in mind. The influence of those strange figures, the Hebrew prophets, upon our minds today is an astonishing thing if one contemplates what must have been their relative impressiveness in their own day of empire builders. The power of Christ in history is the most obvious example of God's persuasion of men. True it is that God has chosen "the weak things of the world that He might put to shame the things that are strong." It has been so in the past with remarkable regularity. It will be so in the future. Let not that be taken as a promise that any particular center of military and political power will be overthrown before it has worked havoc—even spiritual havoc—on a vast scale or that in the divine economy there is no place for the meeting of power with power. That is a problem that I shall discuss in another context. What we can build upon that conviction is the confidence that the cumulative and constructive forces which will outlast all centers of power are those which are typified by these weak instruments of God's persuasion, by the cross followed by the resurrection.

There is interesting confirmation of this faith in some words of Bertrand Russell, who writes from quite a different point of view. He says: "If I had to select four men who have had more power than any others, I should mention Buddha and Christ, Pythagoras and Galileo. No one of these four had the support of the State until after his propaganda had achieved a great measure of success. No one of the four had much success in his own lifetime. No one of the four would have affected human life as he has done if power had been his *primary* object."[10]

4. *God is the redeemer.* The redeeming love of God has always been associated with the divine forgiveness. From one point of view the forgiveness of God is the crown of His righteousness. We know that, even among men, forgiveness is not in conflict with morality but that it represents the highest form of human goodness. We see no incongruity between the willingness to forgive any injury to oneself and personal rectitude. If God were not willing to forgive, He would actually be less righteous than the men whom we most admire. And yet, that is not the end of the matter. There are at least two other considerations which make God's forgiveness the great paradox that Christian theology has usually counted it to be. From the point of view of the sinner who is forgiven it is a paradox. It is easier for an injured person of magnanimous temper to forgive than it is for the person who has done the injury to believe that he is forgiven or to overcome his own sense of guilt. Also, in the case of any private individual who forgives a wrong done to himself there can be concentration upon his personal relations with the offender without necessarily a responsibility to preserve the moral order, and yet, even in the case of personal relations, the individual who is wronged may have to act to protect society in such a way as he would not act if he had to consider only his own attitude toward the offender. But God is not a private individual; He sustains the moral order.

You may think that I am now getting ready to en-

[10] *Power*, pages 271–272.

ter into the discussion of some legal theory of the atonement, which would have come naturally from an orthodox theologian in the middle of the last century. All I care to suggest is that the legal theories of the atonement were ways of underlining a paradox that is still with us when we contemplate the forgiveness of God. I do not believe that any of those theories made the paradox less difficult for the mind to accept. In fact they added fresh complications which made it more difficult to see one's way through the intellectual problem involved.

The paradox, simply stated, is this. Christianity is a religion of the most exacting morality ever taught by man, morality that extends to the depths of human motive. It demands a degree of sensitivity and commitment that we find staggering. God is the God of righteousness. We know Him most clearly when we seriously face the moral demands that life makes upon us and realize that those demands are nothing less than God's demands. That is one side of the paradox. The other side is that Christianity has at its heart the promise that no matter how much we may become involved in disobedience, no matter how long our record of deliberate wrongdoing, it is always possible, if we are honest with ourselves and with God, to turn and be changed. We can begin again without a crippling sense of guilt and without thinking of ourselves as under condemnation. And all of this is true without in the least lowering the moral demand made upon us from the first and without in any way altering the fact that this is a universe in which the most important thing about any one of us is our obedience to the divine righteousness.

Not only is it true that the righteous God does not deal with us in terms of a hard legalism; it is also true that He seeks to save those who are lost. "I say unto you, that even so there shall be joy in heaven over one sinner that repenteth, more than over ninety and nine righteous persons, who need no repentance." This possibility of divine forgiveness, upsetting all legalistic calculations, has gradually dawned upon men through the process of divine revelation and human response that we find in the Bible. In Christ's teaching and in his behavior we see it most clearly and yet without any loss of the element of divine judgment. Doctor Arthur Cushman McGiffert, in his *The God of the Early Christians,* shows conclusively that Jesus' teaching concerning forgiveness in no way superseded the emphasis upon divine judgment.[11] Jesus chose a different kind of sinner for judgment from those emphasized by conventional Judaism, the sinner who in his respectability and pride and callousness was unlikely to be brought to repentance. Repentance which was shown in the willingness to forgive others seemed to be the only condition for forgiveness laid down by Jesus. The effect of Christ's life and death as they have been interpreted by the apostles and by Paul in particular has been to mediate in a new way the forgiveness of God to humanity. This was in line with Christ's own teachings and with his own understanding of God's love for lost souls.

We have seen the gospel of forgiveness neglected by the liberal churches for a generation. This has been

[11]Chapter 1. In rereading the Gospels in the light of this chapter I was surprised to discover that the passages concerning judgment very much outnumber those which emphasize love and forgiveness.

the case for good reasons and for bad. It was a reaction against the one-sided individualistic gospel of forgiveness that seemed to provide too simple a short cut to salvation. It was a reaction against the inadequacy of the legal theories of the atonement by which the paradox of forgiveness was rationalized by orthodox theologians. But it was also the result of a far too simple interpretation of the human situation, an interpretation that missed the depth of human sin and tragedy and the common human need of reconciliation to the source of life's healing and life's peace.

I suggest that there are at least two reasons for a renewed emphasis upon the forgiveness of God. The first is that we have come to see, with the help of the depth psychology and its uncovering of the unconscious elements in the mind, the pervasiveness of the sense of guilt in human life. Some of us know that we are haunted by the memory of particular offenses against honesty, loyalty, and love. Others of us drag around a vague sense of unworthiness—something other than a desirable humility—a defeating sense of unworthiness that casts a shadow on every new start which we may attempt to make in life. The world is full of restless people, driven by some such sense of unworthiness of which they are only dimly conscious and which they would never think of interpreting in theological terms. They seek to escape from themselves into distractions, opiates, busyness and even into mental illness. Anton Boisen in his book *The Exploration of the Inner World* says after a careful study of hundreds of cases in mental hospitals: "To have that in one's life which cannot be brought before his eyes without condemnation is the essence of what we know as the sense of guilt and the source of most mental illness of the functional variety."[12] Our fathers had a resource that most of our contemporaries do not have. They may have overemphasized it and neglected other aspects of the Christian religion, especially its imperative of social justice; but they were able to know in a vivid way the forgiveness of God. Their descendants often must be content to seek a kind of social substitute for forgiveness mediated to them by the psychiatrist. But continuing mental health will often depend upon one's faith that the mercy of God, without cancelling God's moral demand, makes it possible to live with oneself without self-deception and without despair.

The second reason for returning to the Christian gospel of forgiveness is that we find ourselves in a society in which it is often possible for us to make no good choice. I shall have to postpone discussion of this until a later chapter, but here it is important to point out that to live in a world like ours without self-deception and without despair requires now something of the same healing for the soul that individuals must have in their private lives. Our public choices are our personal choices and our public sins are felt by the individual conscience. Do you not respond to these words of T. S. Eliot written after the Munich Conference of 1938? We might apply them to something closer to our own area of responsibility than that conference. "I believe that there must be many persons who, like myself, were deeply shaken by the events of September 1938, in a way from which one does not

[12]Page 173.

recover. . . . The feeling which was new and unexpected was a feeling of humiliation, which seemed to demand an act of personal contrition, of humility, repentance, and amendment; what had happened was something in which one was deeply implicated and responsible."[13] There the sense of social guilt finds honest expression. But how much more often it is smothered and turned into a fanatical defense of policies that one cannot defend with full honesty. Do you not see the world as a place where millions of men are struggling to keep their self-respect without admitting the evil in their hearts and without facing honestly the evil in their collective decisions? Men struggle against their enemies as the only sources of evil because they do not really know themselves and out of that struggle comes all manner of hatred and cruelty. They do not know themselves and they cannot face the worst in themselves, for they do not believe in forgiveness. It is against the background of the divine judgment combined with the divine mercy that men can come to see good and evil with clarity and confront the evil in themselves with honesty. It is one of Reinhold Niebuhr's finest insights that, in the wars and social struggles of our time, the consciousness of being forgiven, following a realistic facing of one's own sin, is the one thing that can prevent self-righteous fanaticism.[14] That this is no academic idea but one that can have meaning in wartime can be seen from the following quotation from Doctor J. H. Oldham published in *The Christian News-Letter:*

[13]*The Idea of a Christian Society,* page 65.
[14]*An Interpretation of Christian Ethics,* Chapter 8.

"Penitence involves more than a general acknowledgment that all nations are sinful. It involves a discrimination between the good and evil elements in our own community and penitence for blindness to the evil. It also means acknowledgment of the good, as well as resistance to the evil, in the enemy. It means, moreover, that if our two goods are to be combined against our common evil we must begin with our own disinfection from the common poison before expecting it in the other. Forgiveness as we now can see must be more than forgetting past wrongs; it involves a definite restoration of a cooperative relationship. It means readiness to say to the party which has immediate responsibility for injury: 'though you have done wrong you are not therefore wholly evil; nor are we wholly good because we have withstood your evil. You are now, upon acknowledgment of your evil, as fit as we are, with the acknowledgment of ours, to cooperate in making our common life anew.' "[15]

[15]November 1, 1939. For information concerning this publication see page 190.

CHAPTER THREE

MAN AND HIS POSSIBILITIES

IT IS natural in times like these that we should come to rethink our ideas about human nature and human possibilities. We have lived through a period during which men have entertained more extravagant hopes concerning their future in this world than has ever before been the case. The idea of indefinite human progress and the faith that by education and by the reform of institutions men could live rationally in a rational society were never widespread until the rise of modern science and particularly until the eighteenth century.

We in America inherited this faith in progress and in essential human rationality and goodness from the thinkers of the eighteenth-century enlightenment, and we added to their doctrines the sense of the plasticity of the human situation that came from experience of the rapid development of a civilization in a wilderness. Before the First World War our expectations for humanity reached the dizziest heights conceivable and even in the period between the two World Wars we maintained the same expectations, sometimes in terms of the gradualism of the educationalists and the religious liberals and sometimes in terms of a confidence in the results of revolution, at least in Russia. American intellectuals until the days of Munich and perhaps even until the days of the German-Russian pact seemed to be able to preserve this optimism concerning man.

An extraordinary degree of disillusionment followed, expressed perhaps most sharply in the writings of Waldo Frank and Lewis Mumford.[1] Even before this disillusionment became general one found such statements as the following in unexpected places. Malcolm Cowley, one of the editors of *The New Republic,* in an article about the Moscow trials said: "Communism has developed its saints and its sacred texts, its doctrinal quarrels and its tragic sense of life. But it has failed to develop the feeling of human limitations, the personal humility that distinguished the Christian ideal at its best. It has failed to give a warning against pride —in Christian theology the sin of the angels, for which Lucifer was cast out of heaven."[2]

American Christians have gone through a similar development. We shared most of the expectations that were characteristic of our society in general and sometimes we gave to them a Christian baptism. We saw the human situation deteriorate, to use an understatement sometimes applied by our diplomats to international relations. In 1932 Reinhold Niebuhr startled

[1]Waldo Frank, *Chart for Rough Water,* and Lewis Mumford, *Faith for Living.* Articles by Lewis Mumford and Waldo Frank in *The New Republic,* April 29, and May 6, 1940.

[2]*The New Republic,* May 25, 1938.

the Church in America by publishing a book with the provocative title: *Moral Man and Immoral Society.* The title was misleading because it suggested that man as such is moral but that he is corrupted by social relations or institutions, an idea that was far from Niebuhr's intention. He saw in the relations between large-scale social groups the most acute form of the human problem, but the source of the problem was to be found in the pride and egoism of man himself. That book of Niebuhr's aroused great resentment among the religious liberals in this country because of its pessimism. If those who resented it were to reread it today they would discover that in comparison with what has actually taken place Niebuhr's pessimism was mild indeed. Niebuhr's thought, if studied as a whole, is extraordinarily balanced, though its dialectical form makes him in any one chapter, article, or speech seem extreme. This is aggravated by the fact that he thinks polemically. In this country Niebuhr has been the spearhead of a new tendency toward what is often called "realism" among American religious thinkers. More effectively than any one else in America he mediates to us insights that are common assumptions in European theology and he does so with moderation.

This tendency toward realism began among theologians about five years before it began among the intellectuals represented by *The Nation* and *The New Republic.* There was a good reason for this more rapid development of realism among Christian thinkers. They had only to consult Christian theology to find a sound basis for it. As members of the world Church they had to pay some attention to European theological developments and thus they were led to rediscover forgotten elements in their own tradition, just such elements as Malcolm Cowley points to in the quotation which I have given.

There is a Christian conception of human nature and human possibilities which transcends our optimistic and pessimistic fashions of thought. It makes full room for the truth in both. Since they are human, Christian thinkers are usually unable to do justice to the balanced character of the Christian view of man. The circumstances of their lives lead them to overemphasize one side or the other, but the balance is soon redressed as circumstances change. A recent reviewer of a book on contemporary religious thought makes this remark: "Although this was perhaps not his intention, the author has shown that the form of religious thinking is just as subject to changing fashions as is the cut of clothing or style of houses, and just as irrelevant to anything permanent in life."[3] I can understand that statement. An outsider reading the articles in *The Christian Century* on how minds have changed during the past decade might well get that impression. It would be more correct to say that fashions in religious thought change—not as fashions in clothes—but as fashions in secular thinking. If changes in fashions discredit religious thinking, they also discredit secular thinking. But what is not seen when you approach Christianity from the outside is that at the heart of it there is a balanced view of human life that constantly corrects one-sided aberrations. It should save us from sentimentalism and cynicism

[3] *Reader's Observer,* July, 1940.

alike. It should keep us from surprise when we find among people humble loyalty and devotion, goodness that is not corrupted by pride, and it should prepare us for the shock when we find men controlled by pride and greed and the lust for power. Let me try now to sketch the outlines of this Christian understanding of man.

The Christian understanding of man consists primarily of the following two affirmations: First, that man is made in the image of God; and, second, that man is a fallen creature. Historically those two affirmations have been carried by a scheme of doctrine which is now untenable. This scheme involved belief in the creation of the original man in a state of perfection and in his fall as an event in time. Our knowledge of the development of man leaves no place for such a perfect state or for such an event as the fall. Moreover, the idea of the fall from a state of perfection is a psychological monstrosity. It is quite true that instead of a fall there has been a rise and indeed a most astonishing rise from the simplest form of life to man as an intelligent and responsible being. But though this development has been a rise the old doctrine of the fall from a perfect state was not without its truth. Professor Brunner in his book on *Man in Revolt* states this truth more persuasively than any one else whom I know. He says that the belief in the fall from a state of perfection as an event in the life of Adam actually obscures the real meaning of the doctrine. It draws the most significant line, so far as unredeemed man is concerned, between Adam as he was before the fall and Adam and all of his unhappy descendants after the fall. Adam was made in the image of God. He lost that image and we, with a few qualifications, start only with his loss. But the real truth of the matter is that all men are made in the image of God and all men are fallen creatures. The contrast is within us and not between Adam as he was before the fall and all humanity since that catastrophic event. It is a permanent contrast—or to use Brunner's stronger word, contradiction—within human life everywhere and at all times. Now, I believe that Brunner himself in his strict adherence to the theology of the Reformation falsifies the situation by assuming that sin completely destroys the content of our original humanity, though the form, understood chiefly as responsibility, remains. This distinction between form and content is a device which enables him to reconcile his position with his chosen theological authorities. He avoids the extreme position of Barth which leaves no place for natural theology and finds a point of contact between revelation and the natural man but still leaves us with a one-sided theory concerning human nature.

Let me state as concisely as possible what these two great affirmations about man may mean to us, even as descriptions of us.

1. Man is made in the image of God.

This affirmation means that man is not primarily an animal or a machine, that he is not fully controlled by his environment or by his heredity, that whatever may be said about the age-long argument over determinism versus indeterminism, man is controlled by his own purposes as well as by his glands, by his vision of the future as well as by the push of the past. Man is a responsible being called by God to free obedience but capable of resisting the call. Man is a rational being, who asks questions without limit (beginning very early in life), who is capable of understanding to an amazing degree the universe which he inhabits and to some degree himself, who develops systems of consistent thought, who develops orders of society and cumulative cultures. Man is a creative person and usually he is miserable if he is not creating or at least playing at creating. His powers of creating are derived, not self-sufficient, but there are areas of his own life where God's creation must be unfinished or frustrated without man's own creative work. There is an infinite restlessness about man, for he never knows long periods of contentment. He supposes that he will be happier after the next thing is accomplished but he soon learns that that is not to be. This restlessness, as Pascal has emphasized, is the burden of his finitude but it is also a suggestion of his relation to the infinite. Man's nature contains impulses of generosity and self-giving which sin does not normally destroy. But above all, man is made for the highest and unless his nature is deadened it cannot find satisfaction except in the highest. As Kierkegaard says over and over again, men can will the good with a single mind but they cannot will the evil with a single mind—at least not without self-deception. As Berdyaev says: "The greatest mystery of life is that satisfaction is felt not by those who take and make demands but by those who give and make sacrifices."[4] As Augustine says: "Thou hast made us for thyself and our hearts are

[4] *The Destiny of Man,* p. 180.

restless till they find their rest in thee."[5] In one of W. E. Orchard's finest prayers there are these words: "We thank Thee that Thou dost never withdraw Thyself from us without our knowing that the Spirit of God has departed."[6] "For whosoever would save his life shall lose it; and whosoever shall lose his life for my sake and the gospel's shall save it" (Mark 8:35). It says a great deal about man to say that he is made that way.

On this side one other thing should be added. Christian theology has never been pessimistic about what God can do with man, though some forms of theology seem to have assumed that the social order is too much even for God. But it is important to point out in these days that the two theologians who are usually regarded as the fountain-heads of Christian pessimism—Paul and Augustine—believed that men by the grace of God can become new creatures. The sixth and eighth chapters of Romans leave no uncertainty about Paul's high expectations concerning the redeemed man. It is a mistake to read the seventh chapter with its classical description of the psychology of sin without the chapters that precede and follow it. "How can we live in sin any longer, when we have died to sin?" "So you must consider yourself dead to sin and alive to God in Christ Jesus our Lord." "But now being made free from sin and become servants to God, ye have your fruit unto sanctification, and the end, eternal life." "For the law of the Spirit of life in Christ Jesus made me free from the law of sin and of

[5]*Confessions,* Book I, Chapter 1.
[6]*The Temple,* page 35.

death" (Romans 6:2, 11, 22; 8:2). Declarative sentences and exhortations succeed one another but both presuppose high possibilities. Augustine was willing to admit that men may approximate perfection; he was concerned to deny only that they can do it without divine grace. Especially in his treatise entitled: "On Man's Perfection in Righteousness"[7] he emphasizes this possibility.

Now, put beside this belief in what man may become by grace a further belief which may come more naturally to us than to Paul or Augustine, that divine grace is available, that it is not limited to the approved ecclesiastical channels nor to an elect minority, that it is effective as an influence making for growth, inspiration, and healing even when it is not recognized as grace at all. Some concession to this truth was made in the doctrines of restraining grace and common grace. As Umphrey Lee suggests in connection with John Wesley,[8] the natural man is an abstraction of theologians. All doctrines of exclusive grace or exclusive revelation are presumptuous in that they set limits to God's activity in the interests of internal theological consistency. Those who live in His world cannot easily escape all the effects of His redeeming influence. As John Oman says, God is no "parsimonious deity."

From the perspective of the inner life of any one of us it is important that we recognize that what good there is in us is a gift, that our very powers are derived, that all is of grace. If we fail to recognize that

[7]*Nicene and Post-Nicene Fathers,* Volume 5.
[8]*John Wesley and Modern Religion,* page 125.

such is the case, we are tempted to become complacent and self-righteous and our very moral achievements become corrupted at their center. One of the chief concerns of all profound theology has been to warn against this danger of self-righteousness. But, when we are estimating objectively the possibilities of moral achievement in the world, when we are estimating the resources which are present in history for the good life, this consideration is most obviously an abstraction. From this point of view our hope must always be in God's grace plus the possibilities in man—man who never becomes himself until he is devoted to the highest. The difference between these two perspectives is not unlike the difference between our judgment of ourselves and our judgment of others. We know some persons whom we admire with few qualifications. Their humble and courageous goodness shows us the possibilities in human life. Even their faults are the other side of their virtues and we would not have them much different. But we could not say this if we knew that they thought in the same way about themselves. I believe that it is in this quite practical way that we should take the warnings against moralism and the emphasis in this theological context on a religious in contrast to a moral dimension.

Turn now to the second affirmation—that man is a fallen creature, a sinner. A few years ago it would have been necessary to elaborate this point more than it is today. We are all much more conscious of the depth, the universality, and the stubbornness of evil in human life than was the case a few years ago. Two factors, in particular, seem to have prepared our minds to perceive the fact of sin. One is the influence of Freudian psychology and other forms of so-called "depth psychology" which concentrate on the irrational and egoistic forces below the threshold of human consciousness. It should be said that this type of psychology also shows the importance of the conscience, however the conscience may be labelled or explained. The other factor which prepares us to see the evil in our midst is the course of events of the past ten years. It is interesting that such an observer as Bertrand Russell, who has long since discarded the conception of sin and who now refrains from using the word, actually finds in human life the same tendency which Reinhold Niebuhr regards as the quintessence of sin. He says: "Every man would like to be God, if it were possible; some few find it difficult to admit the impossibility."[9]

Now, there are many difficulties involved in locating the precise center of sin or in defining sin. There is not space here to enter into a discussion of them. From one point of view the most sinful conduct in the world is that for which we are morally responsible to the full extent. From another point of view, sin is thought of as idolatry and the more complete the idolatry, the more serious the sin, but also the less the moral responsibility, for the man who gives himself with greatest abandon to some ideal or cause or group which is less than God is so blinded that he probably does not know that he is an idolater.[10] But I will leave

[9]*Power,* page 11.

[10]The contrast is most complete in the discussions of the nature of sin in F. R. Tennant's *Concept of Sin* and in Reinhold Niebuhr's *An Interpretation of Christian Ethics,* Chap-

this difficulty. What we do know is that there is a tendency in all of us to look at the world from the point of view of our own interests or of the social interests that are closest to ourselves, that it is difficult not to give priority to the desires that are most vivid because they are our own or, on a higher level, to the desires of the social group which is an extension of ourselves. This tendency toward egoism is in the line of least resistance in human life and is probably the chief root of all the evil that comes into the world through human action.

I believe that we should reject any thoroughgoing doctrine of original sin which is based upon many facts but which blinds us to many other facts. Especially should we be cautious in deducing from such a doctrine other doctrines such as the belief in the inability of man to have any knowledge of God apart from revelation. Egoism in the form of greed, or pride, or the lust for power, is not the only tendency in human nature. I cannot fail to be as much impressed by the goodness of people as I am by the evil in them; and even the evil seems more often to be weakness or moral inertia rather than unlimited pretension. It is very hard to evaluate goodness in a context that is evil; in particular, the simple loyalty and heroism among masses of people who, blinded by propaganda and censorship, are instruments of aggression. Those who insist that there are no degrees of sin or of humble goodness draw a caricature of man. Also, we are in-

---

ter 3. I have dealt with the problem in my chapter in *The Christian Faith and the Common Life* by Nils Ehrenström and others.

clined to become panicky because of the peculiar destructiveness of evil in the world today, but the degree of the external destruction is no real measure of the degree of the evil in the hearts of men. Our deeds are more ghastly than our fathers' deeds without our being worse men than our fathers, because of the instruments of destruction and repression in our hands and the tendency of all evil to spread in an interdependent world. Also, we are trapped in a vicious circle into the making of which have gone the cumulative effects of the evil choices of many generations.

I am not seeking to make out a case for human complacency but merely to keep the picture from being too distorted by the pressure of the immediate situation and to suggest that our thinking about original sin be kept under empirical criticism. I have no doubt but that the great Christian thinkers have been right who have emphasized the depth, the universality, and the permanence of human sin.

There is another area in which the Christian conception of man preserves a balance between extremes. It is in the controversy between those who stress the individual and those who stress the community. In so far as there is an ideological conflict underlying the present war it can be seen most clearly in this area. Karl Polanyi in his illuminating essay on the sources of the philosophy of National Socialism emphasizes the fact that the key to National Socialism as a world view is its complete rejection of the significance of the individual as a person. He points out that there is a close correlation between individualism and universalism, between respect for the individual as a person and concern for all humanity as the ultimate moral unit. He quotes Alfred Rosenberg, the Nazi philosopher, to the effect that "the ultimate antagonism in philosophy is that between the racial-national principle on the one hand, the individualist-universalistic principle on the other."[11] Aurel Kolnai in his book on National Socialist philosophy entitled *The War Against the West* confirms this judgment. He says: "The philosophers and prophets of Naziism are more assiduous in heaping their obloquies on 'individualism' than on any other feature of the West."[12] How far National Socialism on the philosophical level has been accepted by the younger generation of Germans and how far that acceptance has survived the disillusionment of the pact with Bolshelvism, the great target of the philosophy, I do not know. But this anti-individualism, or one might say this anti-personalism, is so consistent with the actual social structure of the National Socialist state that at least we have here ideas that will be learned by regular practice. It is of the utmost importance that we think clearly here, else we may be maneuvered into the defense of an untenable individualism.

The present revulsion against individualism is in part quite consistent with Christianity. Individualism in the search for truth can easily become absurd, for truth is prior to the individual. He must yield to the object and he must do so in cooperation with his fel-

[11]Essay in *Christianity and the Social Revolution,* ed. by Lewis, Polanyi and Kitchin, page 388.

[12]Page 64.

lows who are confronted by the same object. National Socialism is of no help here as it substitutes a national or racial subjectivism for the individualistic subjectivism that may have been the weakness of the West. The clearest thinkers among liberal Christians have known all along the folly of individualistic subjectivism. One of the profoundest statements of the problem is to be found in John Oman's *Grace and Personality,* in which he shows that only when the individual is most true to the demands of objective reality can he be true to himself. As he says, "Only by being true to ourselves can we find the reality we must absolutely follow; yet only by the sense of a reality we must absolutely follow can we be true to ourselves."[13] So Christian individualism is not subjectivism in relation to the truth.

Moreover, Christian individualism is not in any sense the irresponsible individualism that leads to social disintegration. The individual is responsible to God and he is responsible for his fellows. Brunner in his extensive studies of the Christian doctrine of man has set forth this fact of being in a state of responsibility to God as the most characteristic element in human nature. There is nothing in common between the economic individualism of an advanced capitalism and Christian individualism. I do not say that even economic individualism is entirely without truth. There is a point at which individual property rights are very close to the basic rights of a human being, but when that is recognized it must be said immediately that the very truth in economic individualism should drive

[13]Page 66.

Christians to seek a society in which individuals of all classes have property rights. In our time the truth in economic individualism has been used to buttress property rights which have little or no moral justification but which on the contrary are the means by which the owners of capital can preserve power over those dependent upon them for jobs. It is used also to buttress the immoral doctrine that the only guide for production and distribution should be the chance to make profit in an open market, regardless of real human needs not backed by purchasing power and regardless of the use to which the product is put. The *reductio ad absurdum* of this doctrine of the moral neutrality of all exchange of goods and services (that "business is business") has been the sale of arms to aggressors or to enemies or potential enemies by producers in England and France and the United States.

Over against irresponsible individualism and over against the individualism of developed capitalism we find that Christians and fascists of various kinds make many of the same protests. The emphasis upon the community as prior to the individual is a commonplace of social psychology. The emphasis upon the responsibility of the individual to the community as a fellowship of persons is a commonplace of Christian ethics. Without such responsibility Christian love is meaningless.

But when all has been said on that side, there is a Christian individualism which calls for emphasis, a Christian individualism linked with Christian universalism, for obviously we can make no racial or national distinctions in our respect for individual persons.

Let us see some of the grounds for Christian individualism and its essential characteristics.

In the Hebrew background of Christianity we see the roots of Christian individualism, for the prophets frequently defended the rights of the individual against the authority of the king. T. H. Robinson in his discussion of that remarkable episode in which the prophet Nathan condemns King David for his treatment of Uriah and says to the king, "Thou art the man," makes this judgment: "To the ordinary eastern mind, for a king to take the wife of a subject is quite normal and natural, for the sovereign is well within his rights. Few men in David's position would have felt it necessary either to conceal the act or to get rid of the husband. But in Israel a man was a man, even though he were a subject and of foreign birth, and his rights in property and person must be respected. Characteristic also are the rebuke of Nathan and the repentance of the king."[14]

The Christian doctrine of immortality in contrast to all pantheistic ideas underlines the permanent worth of the individual before God. Christianity is necessarily personalistic at this point whether or not one accepts the metaphysics of idealistic personalism.

Again, there is at the heart of Christianity a concern for what one may call the marginal individual, the lost sheep, the anonymous victims who are hungry or naked or in prison, the publicans and sinners who are beyond the pale. Berdyaev says that morality begins when God says to Cain, "Where is thy brother Abel?" and that morality reaches its fulfillment when

[14] *The History of Israel,* page 225.

God says to Abel, "Where is thy brother Cain?"[15] There have been forms of Christian theology that have taught a doctrine of election which would suggest that at least for God there are lost sheep to be accepted as such forever. But fortunately for all such doctrines, now happily out of favor, there was no sure way by which one could tell who the elect and the non-elect were and so it was incumbent on the Christian to treat all persons as though they were elect. The doctrine of election which might seem to set up a cosmic system of persecution of minorities (or was it majorities?) actually undergirded respect for all individuals as, for all one knew, the elect of God.

Perhaps the most important Christian guarantee of individualism lies in the simple fact that while for Christianity the individual is responsible to the community, he is responsible to more than one community. Many lines of responsibility, loyalty and love intersect within the individual. One might even define the individual as that point of intersection. The lines of responsibility, loyalty, and love run out toward family, nation, vocational group, Church, humanity as a whole, and all are dependent upon responsibility, loyalty and love directed toward God. "He that loveth father or mother more than me is not worthy of me" (Matthew 10:37). That can be applied to every object of loyalty short of God. The fact that God is the Lord of all humanity should prevent identification of His will with the interests of any group less than humanity. It is this fact, that the individual is owned

[15]Not even Cain is finally beyond the range of God's love. *The Destiny of Man,* page 351.

by no human group in spite of his varying degrees of responsibility to all human groups to which he belongs, which is the most distinctive mark of Christian individualism. Between that view of man and his responsibilities and the view of the National Socialist there must be perpetual conflict.

Not only can we say that there is a conflict between Christianity and National Socialism; we can also affirm that under modern conditions there is a close relationship between Christianity and democracy. This must be said in a guarded fashion. Historically it is not true that Christianity has always implied political democracy. So long as the power of rulers has been limited by commonly accepted traditions, by a Church which reminded them of standards binding upon them, the evils of tyranny were mitigated. The mere fact of distance did much to protect minorities before the day of the airplane and the radio. It has been possible under an authoritarian state to preserve a sense of human dignity. But under present conditions the only alternatives seem to be the totalitarian state, which is unlimited in its control over the individual and minorities and which must always deprive the Church of all freedom to criticize the state on the one hand, and on the other, a society in which government is responsible to the people with the provision of orderly processes by which those in power can be criticized or displaced. It is safe to say with Karl Barth that "it is true a man may go to hell in a democracy, and achieve salvation under a mobocracy or a dictatorship. But it is not true that a Christian can endorse, desire or seek after a mobocracy or a dictatorship as readily as a democracy."[16] Barth even goes so far as to say that we are justified in thinking of the "democratic conception of the state" as a justifiable expansion of the thought of the New Testament.[17] I emphasize Barth's words, which represent his important change of position, because he cannot be accused of the habit of easily identifying Christianity with political systems. On his statement we in America can take our stand.

Not only do Christians have a vital stake in the survival of democracy but also the Christian conception of the human situation seems to fit exactly the needs of democracy. On the one hand the Christian has faith in human possibilities, for he believes that man was made to be responsive to the highest. Without such faith democracy is impossible. On the other hand the Christian should know more realistically than the secular humanitarian the degree to which men are tempted by power and so he can warn that in every situation provision must be made for the criticism, the checking and the displacing of those who exercise power. If this balance implicit in the Christian point of view is upset, two roads to tyranny are opened: the road of cynical pessimism that plans irresponsible power at the center because there is no faith in the people; and the road of careless optimism that trusts without sufficient reservation those to whom power is given.

I cannot imagine a conception of human nature more completely relevant to the needs of our time. There is indeed a contradiction within human life.

[16]*Church and State,* page 90. [17]*Ibid.,* page 80.

From this we may learn *realism* and the ground for *hope.*

I shall conclude this chapter with a brief discussion of the nature of the social hope that is available to us. Here there is certainly need for the modification of the expectations which have been characteristic of liberal Christians in America. It may be unnecessary to say, in view of the rather general change of thought on this matter, that we can no longer identify the Kingdom of God or the ideal of a fully Christian society with any social order which is to be expected in this world. We must admit that there are seemingly inescapable factors which involve a permanent tendency for the life of large-scale institutions and of natural social groups such as the nation or the class to lag behind the highest developments in personal life. This is a position which it is very hard for some of us to accept and so I shall here suggest the reasons for believing it to be true.

1. There is the fact that every generation must face afresh the problem of growing up. This is a hopeful factor in that it prevents rigidity but it also sets limits to cumulative development. Unless it should turn out to be true that in the sphere of character acquired characteristics are inherited, we can expect the development of future generations to be uneven and precarious. There seems to be a tendency, even within the limits of our observation, for children to rebel against the virtues of their parents and for the vitality of a spiritual trend to grow weaker in the course of one or two generations. Moreover, there is the fact that the

very success of a reform will lead those who inherit its results to forget the evils which had been overcome by patient struggle and to fail to guard against their reappearance under new forms. The danger of relapse into old ways is much greater when we are dealing with generations than when we are dealing with individuals.

2. The large-scale group is able to satisfy the higher impulses of men and at the same time channel them in ways that are anti-social in the relationship between groups. It is here that we see the astonishing contrast between what we know of the kindness and loyalty of individuals and the behavior of the nations to which they belong, behavior to which in varying degrees they consent. From the point of view of the inner harmony of the individual life nationalistic loyalty can be as effective as a higher and more inclusive loyalty, perhaps more effective because it is usually more intense. The interests of the group, whether it be a nation or a class can be so easily idealized that only the most wary are proof against the deception, and this is just as true of the class whose interests are identified with law and order and the existing sanctities as it is of the class that identifies the interests which it may seek to realize by revolutionary action with the interests of the whole community. There then follows a divorce between the significance of motives and the significance of overt conduct.

3. The complexity of social problems and the precariousness of all our judgments concerning them seem to have two effects. One is that they lead to inertia or to evasion. Problems remain unsolved and

as a result historical forces are thrown farther out of adjustment. The other effect is that some daring solution may be attempted with the result that the by-products of the solution which may not have been forseen create a whole new set of problems. It is not necessary to be dogmatic and to say as Berdyaev says: "not one single project elaborated within the historical process has ever proved successful."[18] It is not necessary to assume that every advance will be cancelled out by its evil by-products as is now often assumed. But that this tendency is inescapable in the historical process it is difficult to deny.

4. In connection with the relations between social groups the effects of the sin and finiteness of the individual are even clearer than in personal relations. It is very hard to do justice to persons at a distance. Also, we may not realize the *intensity* of their need. It is easy to be so discouraged by the magnitude of their suffering—when they are strange masses—that we seize the nearest excuse for doing nothing. Some of our arguments for doing as little as possible about refugees are illustrations of this. We are preoccupied with the needs which are close to us and have only margins of our time and attention for needs at a distance. The tendency to rationalize the interests of our own group in terms of universal interests renders the situation even more serious. Our passing of responsibility back and forth is one of the ways in which we destroy the edge of all responsibility. The people pass the responsibility to the man-on-the-spot who represents them and the man-on-the-spot passes the responsibility back to

[18]*The Meaning of History,* page 198.

the people. John Foster Dulles has written of those who hold public office: "They are apt to be considered, and to consider themselves, as trustees, not of the general welfare of humanity, but of the particular electoral group they represent."[19]

All that has been said about the universal and permanent character of human sin in the early part of this chapter is reinforced by these four considerations.

Where does this discussion leave us?

There are those who deny the *possibility* of any social hope. They assume that every gain will be balanced by a corresponding loss. They seem to imply that, on the plane of history, the so-called demonic forces must always be equal in strength to the persuasive work of God in history. I fail to see any reason for such an assumption as that. Usually it is deduced from a doctrine which is based upon tradition or upon facts of inner religious experience, or it involves the confusion of the inner check upon self-righteousness with an objective valuation of moral possibilities.

There are those who deny the *importance* of a social hope. They say that man lives for eternity, and they understand eternity either as man's standing before God in each moment of existence or in terms of a hope in an ultimate triumph which will be the end of history, a triumph which will not be affected by any achievements in the world of time. Both of those interpretations of our relationship to the eternal are meaningful but they should not be allowed to exclude emphasis upon the reference to the future in all purposive living. At the present moment we do stand be-

[19]*Religion in Life*. Winter, 1938.

fore God and it is the commitment of our wills to His will that matters most. But the actual content of His will as we understand it in the concrete has a future reference. We cannot begin to know what that will is without using our minds to discover as far as possible the consequences of proposed lines of action. Obedience in the present must necessarily involve purposive action directed toward the future. The charge is often made that stress on the idea of progress means the sacrifice of this and future generations to the generations which will live in some distant golden age. Sometimes the expectation of progress has been emphasized in such a way as to be vulnerable at this point. But this common criticism fails to recognize the degree to which men at their best find meaning for the present from the thought that their work will have desirable consequences in the future.

However, on the side of those who look for a better society in this world there are some who refuse to substitute sober expectations for their romantic dreams. They insist that there can be no incentive for social action at all unless we believe that the Kingdom of God in its fullness will come in history. But surely they are wrong. The primary basis for social responsibility is no such calculation concerning the ultimate prospects for society. Rather, the basis for such responsibility is obedience to the will of God. It may be true, for example, that a particular institution is a blight on the lives of quite definite human beings, human beings who will not be living a hundred years from now. We do not have to know now about the far-off goals of history to know that anti-Semitism is a desecration and that the slaughter of war and the repression of tyranny represent the depersonalization of life and that we have responsibility to overcome these evils at all points where we have any leverage. Our social responsibility differs in form if we are in a concentration camp from what it is if we are citizens of a free nation; it is relative to the degree of our power or our freedom. That would still be true if history were to be ended by a cosmic storm in a thousand years.

But we can say more than this. Social responsibility is not based upon our expectations concerning the distant future but there is added incentive if we can have hope for the future. Is there good reason for denying that the future is open? Can we not live by hope, not hope that this society of ours will be the Kingdom of God, but hope that men may solve the problem of living together in an interdependent world without destroying one another, hope that it may be possible to keep society from anarchy without making men into puppets, hope that we may not be forever helpless in the face of the productivity of the machine, but that we may become able to relate that productivity to human needs? It is not for us to have the comfort of assurance that these things must be. Still less can we have the comfort of assurance that these things will be before present trends have led us into even greater disasters than we have yet known. But the future is open. A world is possible in which there is a structure which will not defeat life and within which individuals and groups, and especially the Christian Church, will be able to rise to high levels without intolerable compromise. This problem of living together in an interdependent world with all the resources of science for creation and destruction in our hands is essentially a new problem and theologians have no right to assert that it cannot be solved.

Moreover, it is becoming increasingly clear that the alternatives are not between solving these central problems and drifting as we have been doing. The alternatives are progress in these areas or barbarism and the kind of barbarism which has all the implements of modern science and which leaves no chance for any one to escape from its control. There is no guarantee of progress in this threat, but there is some hope that it will be the needed spur. God has not abandoned us. He draws us and He punishes us. We cannot say that men in their freedom will not resist Him so stubbornly that there will be centuries of darkness. But it need not be so. And if the worst does come, we can know that there are still in the world quiet and unpretentious forces through which God will continue to persuade us. With these forces we can work now.

I find one of the most satisfactory statements of what we can hope for in society in Jacques Maritain's *True Humanism*. One must make allowance for forms of expression that are not natural to American Protestants. He writes: "The Christian, indeed, is never *resigned*. His conception of the city holds in it of its very nature the wish to adjust the conditions of this vale of tears so as to procure a relative but very real earthly happiness for the assembled multitude; a polity in which all can find a good and decent living, a state of justice, of amity and prosperity making possible for each the fulfillment of his destiny. He claims that the terrestrial city should be so directed as effectively to recognize the right of each of its members to live, to work and to grow in their life as persons."[20] Can any one expect more than this? Should any one expect less?

[20]Page 131.

CHAPTER FOUR

CHRISTIANS IN SOCIETY

IN THE coming period Christians will be tempted to neglect their responsibility as Christians for the institutions of society. They will be tempted to do this because of a quite natural disillusionment concerning all efforts to realize Christian ideals in society. They have championed numerous causes as Christian causes and so many of them have seemed to fail—Prohibition, the League of Nations, the World Court and Disarmament. Those that have not failed have lost some of their glamour as they have attained partial success and have raised fresh problems. For example, the labor movement, which at the very time when the national stage is set for its success, is seriously handicapped by its own divisions and by defects of leadership, defects which are real though exaggerated by the opponents of labor. Also, those who have been in the vanguard of the movement for Christian social action are deeply divided by the problems raised by the war. They have no united voice on the issue of intervention versus pacifism and no confident voice on the subject of conscription. The social idealists outside the Church are much confused by the same disappointments and the same divisions.

We in the Church may be tempted to neglect our responsibility for social institutions for another reason. It is the fact, already mentioned in the first chapter, that the Church outside of America may have little or no freedom to speak about social institutions. This may lead to a wave of individualistic and otherworldly Christian thinking, the contagion of which will be hard to resist, especially as it may fit some of our own moods.

Such a development as this would be no continuation of the trend away from liberalism that has been a marked characteristic of Christian thought for the past twenty years. This trend away from liberalism has not been in the direction of evangelical individualism. Such men as Brunner, Niebuhr, Tillich, Berdyaev, Temple, Maritain represent a profound concern for the problems of society. Even Barth, whose influence has sometimes been on the side of quietism in relation to social issues, has become a crusader for democracy as against National Socialism. Moreover, every one of the great ecumenical conferences of the past twenty years has set forth in emphatic terms the responsibility of the Christian and of the Church for society, and both the Oxford and the Madras Conferences represented very high levels of Christian social insight. So the muffling of Christian social teaching against which I am warning would be no continuation of present trends but a new development. American Christians should resist this development. They have a responsibility to keep alive Christian social teaching not only in their own behalf but in behalf of the world Church. What it may be increasingly difficult for others to say we can still say, and we can say it together with many Christians in nations which retain their freedom who form with us a free nucleus of the world Church.

The fact that we shall be tempted to abandon the social emphasis that has been characteristic of American liberal Christianity makes it timely to consider the basis in the Christian religion of what we have called "the Social Gospel." The Social Gospel has been much criticized in recent years because of its optimistic expectations for society and because of a tendency to identify Christianity too easily with specific political programs and social movements. Christian social teaching in the future must make full allowance for these criticisms, but the Social Gospel at its center represents imperatives that are at the heart of the Christian religion. To neglect those imperatives is a form of apostasy. In this chapter I shall first outline the basis for the Social Gospel and then I shall suggest ways in which Christian social teaching and Christian social strategy should be revised in the light of events and contemporary theological criticisms.[1]

[1]I use the term "Social Gospel" with misgiving because those words suggest a one-sided gospel that is social rather than personal and because they have come to stand for a pattern of thought which needs drastic revision. On the other hand, it is important to preserve the momentum that the impulse behind the Social Gospel has gained. To abandon the words might suggest a break with that impulse and that would be more misleading than to use them.

There are at least four reasons for regarding the Social Gospel as organic to the Christian religion, or, as we might say, four links between the personal and social emphases in Christianity. These four links are themselves closely interrelated. They are really four different ways of approaching the subject. Any one of them is strong enough to hold in spite of all the criticism that can now be brought against older forms of the Social Gospel. I should even maintain that each of them is independent of the controversies among New Testament scholars concerning Jesus' teaching about the Kingdom of God. If Jesus himself related the Kingdom of God to a new social order in this world the relation between the teachings of Jesus and the Social Gospel is more obvious on the surface, but even if Jesus did not himself deal with the political and economic structure of his society we cannot live under the influence of his teachings in our situation without translating them into concern for the political and economic structure of our society.[2]

The links between the social and the personal aspects of Christianity are the following: (1) The social responsibilities of Christian love; (2) the range of

[2]New Testament scholars seem to be as changeable as theologians. They have moved within a little more than a generation from emphasis upon the Kingdom as a present reality or a new order to be developed in this world to emphasis upon the Kingdom as a future order to come by a divine miracle. Now another shift in emphasis is suggested by the writings of C. H. Dodd and Frederick C. Grant. But this new development does not justify our thinking of Jesus' teaching in terms of political action or in terms of participation in the class struggle. In any case I have sought to show that the imperatives of the Social Gospel are necessary extensions of

Christian repentance; (3) obedience to the will of God as the Lord of history; (4) the conditions that are necessary for the freedom of the Church to be the Church. I shall now discuss each of them. It may seem to most readers of this book that such discussion is unnecessary because to them it is all so obvious, but my reasons for presenting it are that we may at any time be under great temptation to abandon emphasis upon the Social Gospel.

1. *The social responsibilities of Christian love.* Christian love necessarily implies concern for the welfare of all groups of persons and especially all groups of persons who are in any way affected by our decisions. It must be remembered that even our political decisions are our decisions as persons. Responsibility for people at a distance, for other classes and races which are affected by what we do or leave undone, is an obvious corollary of love. Sometimes we have debated about how love is related to justice, but while there are important issues at stake in those debates they are often allowed to obscure the main point—

---

the teachings of Jesus, given even the least social interpretation of them. Was not Schweitzer himself, whose interpretation of Jesus' teachings rendered them most remote from the problems of society, sent to Africa under the influence of Jesus? He refers especially to the parable of Dives and Lazarus. Our situation differs from that in which Jesus lived in three important respects. (1) We think in terms of an indefinite future in this world within which we have responsibility for the long-run consequences of our political choices. (2) We have the opportunity to abolish poverty if we choose to organize our economic life for that purpose. (3) Christians in democratic nations in part mould the public opinion on which political choices depend.

that in every situation in which we find ourselves love should will a structure of social justice as the condition which is necessary for all forms of life that are on a higher level than justice.

On one side it is true that justice is the restraint of evil in terms of punishment or in terms of resistance to tyranny or aggression, but these negative aspects receive their meaning from their contribution to positive justice. One of the traditional ways of stating the nature of positive justice, which goes back to the Stoic lawyers and which was taken over by the Christian fathers, is that to do justice is *to give every man his due.*[3] But what is every man's due? What an existing legal system gives him as his due? Obviously not that. Actually this view of justice could be applied to a society divided into masters and slaves for that which was due to each class was determined by law or tradition. I suggest a modification of that ancient formula. Justice on the positive side should be the organization of society in such a way as *to give every child his due.* This means that every child should have the opportunity to develop his capacities without the adventitious handicaps that are the result of the economic condition or social status of his parents. You can say many other things about justice, but if you do not include this in what you say all the rest remains hollow. Justice on the negative side—punishment and resistance to tyranny and aggression—may involve grave problems of compromise for the Christian, though the effort of society to make sure that the innocent are not punished is one aspect of punitive justice that is close

[3]St. Augustine, *The City of God,* Book XIX, Chapter IV.

to the demands of love. The positive side of justice, as I have described it, is merely the translation of Christian love into terms that are relevant to social organization. To realize such justice we must have imagination controlled by the motive of love.

One of the points at which the modern Social Gospel is in advance of earlier Christian teaching is that its representatives have been able to see clearly the ways in which human personality is moulded and often warped by environment, by institutions and economic circumstance. The scientific study of society and modern psychology have demonstrated both the effect of social institutions upon the development of children and the extent to which the adult personality is moulded during the earliest years of childhood. I have stressed the place of children in our social responsibility because in their case one can give full weight to the place of environment without falling into a false environmental determinism. The freedom to rise above all external circumstances can be attained, but we are not born with it and the most impressionable years of our lives are those in which external circumstances are most decisive. There are circumstances in which even the family is no adequate buffer between the child and the world. This is often true under conditions of demoralizing poverty. In quite a different way this is true in those totalitarian societies in which the state seeks to capture the minds of children and to set them against the religious and moral ideals of their parents.

There is another social implementation of Christian love which is new in our time. It arises from the fact that for the first time in history it is possible to produce enough economic goods to abolish poverty. In the face of economic need Jesus could suggest only charity because his society was one in which poverty was inevitable. In our time poverty is not the result of inevitable scarcity that could be attributed to an act of God, but it is the result of a form of social organization that throttles the productive system because it can find no way according to its rules of matching purchasing power with actual economic need. There is one passage in the report of the section on The Church and the Economic Order of the Oxford Conference which seems to me to be a milestone in the thinking of Christians about economic responsibility: After affirming that we now have the technological resources for the abolition of poverty, the report says: "This possibility marks off our time from the period of the New Testament and from other periods in which Christian thinking about economic life has been formulated. In the light of it the direction of Christian effort in relation to the economic order should henceforth be turned from charitable paternalism to the realization of more equal justice in the distribution of wealth."[4] When that idea enters deeply into the consciousness of people in the Church it may prepare their minds to accept the new forms of economic organization which are coming through political pressure from the groups that feel the pinch of this artificial poverty, and it may undercut their tendency to allow philanthropy to satisfy their consciences for per-

[4]Report on "The Church and the Economic Order," Part III. See Bibliographical note, page 152 n.

mitting the situation to exist which makes philanthropy necessary.

2. *The range of Christian repentance.* The gospel is a gospel of repentance but repentance is very narrow and artificial if understood only in terms of our private lives. Is it not obvious that Christian repentance must be based upon moral sensitivity to the behavior of the groups to which we belong, particularly the behavior of the nation of which we are citizens and within which we have a voice in the making of public policy? We are in a position to be more realistic about the demands of Christian repentance than has been usual in Christian circles in the past. We can see with greater clarity than has been the case with previous generations that the acid test of repentance is to be found in our attitude in economic relationships. Jesus saw that this was true when he told the story of Dives and Lazarus and when in the story of the Last Judgment he said that the eternal fate of men depended upon their attitude toward common human need—toward the anonymous victims who were hungry, sick, imprisoned.

Here again a modern insight can extend the range of a Christian imperative. We see more clearly than ever before that our minds are controlled by the interests of the groups to which we belong, especially by their economic interests. We see this clearly in the case of nations, above all in the case of *other* nations, but it is also true of economic classes. I do not mean by "classes" merely the so-called "capitalists" and the "working class." Actually there are many groups whose attitude toward society is determined by some economic interest which unites each group. Farmers may be divided between owners and tenants and even according to their major crops. Skilled workers who have already achieved status and security may be ranged against the new struggles of unskilled workers who are not yet effectively organized. There are often specific issues on which particular professions or particular types of business are determined by some narrow interest. There is a great danger that the clergy, protected by rising standards of entrance to the profession and by provisions for pensions and minimum salaries, may become a class which is determined in its attitude by fear of anything that may disturb its security.

Every Christian should become aware of the factors which determine his judgment, should suspect his own motives because he knows that sin is natural to him, should put the burden of proof on those social judgments which harmonize with the economic interests of his group. The Protestant Churches would do well to concentrate upon the peculiar temptations of the middle classes; for in the case of the middle classes the influence of economic interest is especially subtle and deceptive. It is easy for them to convince themselves that they are the community and that what is good for them is good for the community. Their control over the press, the universities and the churches gives them almost a monopoly of those agencies which mould the climate of opinion. When the opinions that are based upon interest are echoed by what seems to be the opinion of the community, partial interests become disguised as patriotism. The Christian should live under influences which enable him to cut through these false fronts. Until we do so our repentance will not correspond with our real situation.

3. *Obedience to the will of God as the Lord of history.* The Christian's responsibility for the public life of the world is a natural consequence of the fact that God is the Lord of history. He is concerned with the public life of men, with nations and with social movements as well as with the souls of individuals. The Christian religion is not a religion of escape from the world but a religion of obedience to God in the world. The recent revival of a strong emphasis upon social justice in the teachings of the churches is in part the result of a fresh discovery of the Old Testament prophets. Historical study of the prophets reveals them as individual men with distinctive messages for specific social situations, and these messages are saturated with the demand of God for social righteousness.

Jesus stood in the tradition of the prophets. His spirit was nourished by their writings. He shared their concern for the poor and oppressed though his social situation was different from that of the prophets and he may not have dealt directly with the policy of the nation as they did in days of national freedom. His teaching, when implemented realistically in our situation, implies drastic change of our economic and international order as the will of God. As we confront the various forms of exploitation and tyranny and cruelty in the world, we know that it is God's will that we overcome them. Before Him our human distinctions of race and nationality and social status are as nothing. The spectacle of a small number of people in every century appropriating, because of their military, political or economic power, the chief sources of wealth and leaving the masses without the same access that they take for themselves to the means of health and to the opportunities to develop the possibilities within them is in the sight of God a great blasphemy. From this perspective it is entirely false to make a sharp separation between the spiritual and the material. A just distribution of material goods is itself a spiritual ideal and the quest for that justice is obedience to God.

4. *The conditions that are necessary for the freedom of the Church to be the Church.* The Church is not free to be the Church in all environments. It may retain its integrity by going underground but in doing that it is in danger of losing contact with its own youth. It is a common saying that spiritual freedom does not depend upon political liberty. That is quite true for those who already have spiritual freedom, but in our world it may be that without political liberty there will be very few who will be able to attain spiritual freedom. Any one who believes that the Church need not concern itself with more than the saving of individuals must face the fact that a political change which alters the character of the state may make it impossible for the Church to preach the gospel publicly except as it takes over the state's interpretation of the gospel. In our society the Church has sufficient influence now to be one of the chief factors in preventing the development of a totalitarian state. It will serve the cause of human liberty in general if it preserves its own freedom to interpret Christianity to the nation.

I come now to a much more difficult aspect of this

subject. It is easy to show that Christians as Christians have a responsibility for a radical change of social institutions—yes, and also to prevent some kinds of radical change. But when one comes to say by what policies and programs that responsibility should be implemented the ground under our feet becomes more uncertain. Here we find that our social decisions are far more precarious than seemed to be the case a few years ago. Why are they so precarious? I think that the answer is that, while in every important social decision there are moral elements, involving especially motives and consequences for human beings, concerning which we can get guidance from Christianity, there are also, intertwined with those moral elements, three other elements concerning which there is no specifically Christian guidance and about which even the most sensitive Christians may differ. These neutral elements, as I might call them—neutral from the point of view of Christian ethics—are: (1) technical judgments depending upon expert knowledge; (2) the prediction of human behavior that is likely to follow a given policy; (3) the still more difficult problem that arises when we face only evil alternatives and must weigh the consequences of each choice—knowing that all involve tragic evil.

First, consider the technical judgments. One of our difficulties is that the experts differ in their judgments. One pertinent illustration of this is the difference in judgments concerning the best method of securing full re-employment. There are those who sincerely believe that the road to full re-employment is to reduce to a minimum all government regulation of business, to remove burdensome taxes, to return as far as possible to a condition in which there is free enterprise for the businessman so that he may be encouraged by the prospect of large profits to invest and employ and produce. It is assumed that if this is done there will be such a volume of employment that the market for the goods that are produced will automatically follow from the distribution of income accompanying the process. Together with this general prescription there is usually a warning against monopoly prices and high tariffs. On the other hand, there are experts who believe that the problem of re-employment cannot be solved by any such means, that such means suggest a return to the condition of the 1920's which led to the great depression, that direct attempts by government must be made to raise the purchasing power of the masses of the people to provide a market for the goods that can be produced, that private investment must be supplemented on a large scale by public investment, that, as unplanned business enterprise under present conditions can never employ the full productive capacity of the nation, the path of advance must necessarily be through the increase of the role of the government as the organ of the community in economic life.

I enlarge on this conflict of views on what are essentially technical economic issues because I desire to point out one very important fact about technical issues. They can often be used as a façade for special interests. It is not strange that the first philosophy of economic advance is today loudly advocated by most businessmen—with some tendency to forget what is an essential part of the prescription, the warning against monopoly prices and high tariffs. That part of the prescription that fits economic interests is devoutly believed as though it were a matter of objective science. It is necessary to distinguish between the businessman or industrialist as an expert concerning a particular process of production and distribution and the businessman or industrialist as a member of a class whose interests are involved in the maintenance of as much free enterprise as possible. The second philosophy of economic advance is usually advocated by the spokesmen of labor and some parts of it appeal to farm groups. That philosophy is in harmony with the economic interests of those classes. What I want to emphasize is that there is involved here a technical issue which Christians as Christians cannot settle, but that it is clear that technical issues never come pure in these matters and that it is well to be on one's guard against the claims of the expert in so far as his conclusions *fit the economic interests of the class which supports him and within which he moves.* To say the least the expert whose theories harmonize with the interests of one economic class must be corrected by reference to the experts whose theories fit the interests of other classes. Christians, if they are aware of this situation, can keep their discussion on a level of greater tolerance and, because they are on their guard against the ways in which their own minds are corrupted, can correct their own judgments.

The Church should concentrate attention on the effects of any policy upon persons and remind all kinds of experts of the most important human facts by which their theories must be tested. At this point the clergy have a distinctive contribution to make. They are relatively independent of the pressures of group interests. This may prevent them from understanding the situation precisely as it appears to each of the groups involved, but their very detachment makes possible a form of wisdom that is much needed to keep attention focussed on the true ends of all economic processes and for mediation between the parties in conflict.

The second element—social prediction—raises much the same kind of neutral problems for Christian ethics as technical judgments. The chief difference is that in this area we have less knowledge and all of our assumptions are more precarious. It is difficult to say who is an expert here. History, sociology and psychology may contribute most to such expertness but they are stretched when used in this way beyond the possibility of controlled methods of enquiry. Yet, this area of social prediction is often decisive. Discussion of foreign policy for some years has consisted quite largely in an attempt to guess what Hitler or the Japanese militarists will do next if we take a certain kind of action. Most of our arguments about the methods and tempo of economic change presuppose assumptions concerning the psychology of various social classes, an area in which dogmatism seems to be easy but where knowledge is very limited. It is important to realize that these problems of social prediction are often introduced into what appear to be technical discussions and the results are not recognized to be as precarious as they really are. For example, discussions of possible economic systems are often based upon the assumption that we already know enough about human motivation. The conservative often assumes that the profit motive is the mainspring of human enterprise and he fails to do justice to the extent to which men may be controlled by the desire for social approval and by idealistic motives. The radical often assumes that human motivation will take care of itself when once we get a rational economic order and he fails to realize how easy it will be to fall into inertia or to yield to temptations to abuse power when the early enthusiasm for the new order fades. The problem of predicting the behavior of human beings in some other society of which we may dream is far more complicated than either side realizes. Christianity, with its view of human nature, can warn against both a cynical and a sentimental conception of human possibilities, but there is no distinctively Christian solution to this problem as we face it in the context of complicated social choices.

By far the most difficult area in which the Christian must make social decisions is where every possible choice is so evil that whatever we do we are involved in a tragic compromise. There is no Christian law which can provide a short cut to decision here. Christians of equal sincerity and sensitivity will inevitably differ, for they will not only interpret the demands of the situation differently because of differences in technical judgment and in social prediction but they will also have varying estimates of the comparative claim of such values as non-violence on the one hand and on the other the prevention or overcoming of tyranny.

There are four possible attitudes which we can take when we face choices of this sort. Actually most political choices are to some degree choices between evils though the differences in degree may be so great as to disguise that fact. I shall discuss each of these possibilities and then consider the issues raised by Christian pacifism, a point of view which appears to cut the most difficult knots and one that is of great importance in current controversies.

1. The first way in which to deal with this problem is to assume that the next best thing which we see to do from the standpoint of its social consequences is the Christian choice, that we are to identify it with God's will for us and enter upon it without serious inner tension. One form that this position takes has much to be said for it. It is the natural assumption that because God must have a will for each situation, the best possible choice that we find available is His will.[5] There are two qualifications which are necessary if this position is to be at all defensible. If these qualifications are emphasized then this position merges into the fourth that will be discussed later. One qualification grows out of the fact that actually we shall find Christians who are equally sincere who deny that our choice is the best possible choice; and their consciences must be respected and they must keep our own consciences under judgment. The other qualification is that God's will in the midst of social conflict can never be identified in a simple way with any one side in the conflict. It is the sins of all of us that are responsible for the conflict and that have created the

[5]This general position is emphasized by D. C. Macintosh (*Social Religion,* page 66) and Archbishop William Temple (*The Christian Faith and the Common Life,* ed. by Nils Ehrenström and others, page 58).

situation which so tragically limits the possibilities open to any of us, and we can know that it will be the sins of the human representatives of what may be a relatively just cause which will in some measure mar the justice of that cause even if it triumphs.

There is another form of this first way of dealing with human choices among evil alternatives which is to be avoided at all costs. It is the tendency to blind oneself to the evil in one's choice and to identify the choice with the will of God without repentance. Here are some sharply contrasting illustrations of this tendency. The Oxford Groups tend to identify their ideal of absolute love and absolute honesty with works of philanthropy which are possible within the present economic order. The Christian Left, a company of Christian Marxists in England not only identified Christianity with the struggle for Socialism (perhaps in itself a good corrective for the almost unconscious identification of Christianity with capitalism which is so widespread) but also linked this struggle closely with the institutions of the Soviet Union. Some of them may be disillusioned now but their experience should be a warning against all such religious idealizations of human systems. Many American pacifists uncritically place the sanction of their absolute behind the policies advocated by the isolationists. Another illustration of this same tendency is the identification of Christianity with the national cause in time of war. The freedom of the Church may be at stake in a war; also the chance for a society to be open to Christian influences may depend upon the outcome. But these external advantages for Christianity will be nullified if they are not accompanied by deep-going national repentance and the habit of keeping national policy under criticism in the light of a standard that transcends the national will.

2. The second position is that which seems to be characteristic of some forms of Lutheranism and which, while far from Barth's present views, was encouraged by Barth's emphasis upon the absolute transcendence of God. It is the view that the Christian standard is so remote from possible realization in this world, especially in society, that its chief function is to convict us of sin and drive us all to seek forgiveness as individuals through faith in the gospel. Sometimes the proclamation of the fact of sin by our contemporaries seems to be a fatalistic summons to men to live down to their reputation as sinners, at least in public life. Christianity of this type leads inevitably to a double standard of personal and social ethics. It abdicates from the task of relevant social criticism and leaves a moral vacuum into which flow whatever ideals happen to be approved by secular society. Those who hold this position make much of Paul's words: "Let every soul be in subjection to the higher powers; for there is no power but of God; and the powers that be are ordained of God." There is here a convenient doctrine of God's providence in society which makes possible service to the most non-moral state with a clear conscience, while the Christian in his own soul is forgiven and knows religious assurance. This use of Paul's words as a law, the effect of which has been incalculable in rendering Christians uncritical of the state, fails to recognize that Paul was writing while the Ro-

man state was on the whole helpful to his cause. After the Neronian persecutions it was not possible to say: "For rulers are not a terror to the good work, but to the evil."[6] The author of the book of Revelation learned that lesson and Karl Barth learned it again recently but it has been too often forgotten.

There has developed in several of the nations at war an attitude that resembles this one in some respects. It is the attitude of those who say the war is a dirty business with which God and Christianity have nothing to do and yet who see no alternative but to participate in it. It is their Christian sensitivity that is largely responsible for their suspension of their Christianity until after the war is over. Those who share this attitude have none of the comfort that comes to Christians who, following Paul's words, make the state the keeper of the conscience in public affairs and continue without interruption their private religious life. This position is well expressed in some words used to suggest the attitude of some of the younger Christians in England: "We must fight this war, but it is a dirty business. And if any Bishop tells us that this is a Christian thing, then let's string up the Bishop."

3. The third position may start with a judgment concerning the unchristian character of all political alternatives which resembles that involved in the second position but its response to this situation is entirely different. It involves detachment from the political policy of the nation, as much detachment as is consistent with positive action on a non-political level. This action is designed to heal the wounds of war and

[6]This whole discussion is based on Romans 13:1–7.

to keep alive a spirit free from hate and unclouded by the falsehood that war breeds. Those who choose this course may seem irresponsible on the political level but they do not withdraw from society; they remain responsible for a kind of social action which in the long run can be expected to raise the level of the political possibilities open to the Christian. They seek to preserve influences of sanity and mercy which will be sorely needed when the crisis is passed, to keep alive bonds of unity that are deeper than politics. I do not believe that it is necessary to be a pacifist in order to have some part in this non-political redemptive activity, for there has developed in this war a form of non-pacifist Christianity, to be described later, which is far in advance of the attitude of the conventional patriot. Still, it is probable that pacifists, if they rise above the temptation to be self-righteous, by their concentration upon this redemptive function can make a contribution that no one else can make.

This position is represented by the Quakers in time of war. In so far as they form part of political pressure groups controlled by the conviction that they have a strategy that the nation must always adopt, their position will be criticized later in this chapter; but in so far as they make the most of non-political means of social redemption in times of crisis, they represent an essential Christian way of life. The policy of the Quakers seems to be abundantly justified by the probability that in a world in which there are no nations that combine neutrality with independence of action and moral prestige the Quakers will be the only people in the world whom every one will trust. They have an advantage in dealing with Germany because of their record after the last war. They may have to pay the price of foregoing verbal denunciations of that which is the absolute antithesis of their own spirit but to allow the antithesis to be observed is more effective.

4. The fourth position is less easily stated than the others because it is essentially dialectical. That is, it preserves within itself a greater degree of tension than the others. It recognizes that Christian love cannot be fully realized in a world of sin. It refuses to identify Christianity with any political policy and in fact draws back from the identification of any policy with the will of God. At least, if it is said that the policy is willed by God, it is necessary to add that even in doing the will of God we are sinners, for it is because of our previous choices that it is impossible to make a good choice now. But those who share this general attitude emphasize in most situations one political policy that on the whole is relatively more just than another. They reject the pacifist absolute and are today found in support of war in China or in England where it is fought against aggression and the extension of tyranny. On the other hand, there is no reason why those who share this position should not in some situations be conscientious objectors against war. But they reject the emphasis upon keeping one's own soul unspotted by violence in disregard of the social consequences of a policy of non-violence on the part of the nation.

The dialectical character of this position is shown by the refusal on the one hand to identify Christianity with political policies and the refusal on the other hand to allow a moral dualism to arise with one standard for private life and another standard for public life. Christian love should control the motives of men in public life. Love must keep every social choice under judgment and drive us to raise the level of possibilities. Our very compromises, instead of being accepted complacently as the result of living in a sinful world, should impel us to create a situation in which they will not be necessary. Doubtless there will be new compromises demanded of us in new situations, but that fact does not destroy our responsibility for seeking to remove the causes of existing compromises.

This is essentially the position held by Reinhold Niebuhr and expressed in his paradoxical statement that love is an "impossible possibility." It is relevant to all of our choices without being fully realized by any of them. Professor Niebuhr seems to me to divert attention from the real center of the difficulty by his extremely perfectionist interpretation of love in terms of complete selflessness and complete non-resistance. His conception of love does not suggest an ideal that has meaning except for the most intimate personal relations. To stress the fact that this kind of love cannot be realized in the world of politics does not point to the most disturbing fact. Far more harassing is the fact, recognized also by Niebuhr, that it is impossible to live fully according to a standard of positive justice so long as one lives in a condition of relative privilege. Also, there is the fact that the demands of negative justice—the necessity of restraining crime or tyranny or aggression—conflict with the demand of positive justice that all persons, especially children, have opportunities to develop their capacities. When the instrument of the blockade is used against innocent masses because it is the only weapon available to curb the power of Hitler, the conflict is not between love in a perfectionist sense and justice, but between what I have called positive justice and what seem to be the demands of negative justice. Can one imagine a more harrowing conflict than that?

The conflict will not be essentially altered in principle if ways are found to mitigate the effects of the blockade on the conquered countries, for, if the blockade succeeds, innocent Germans will starve later. I do not say this in order to suggest that the blockade should be abandoned, for the alternative would be actually worse if it meant the consolidation of Nazi power, but to illustrate the real nature of the conflict between all that we usually associate with human decency, not to speak of love, and the demands of negative justice. That the British government is very sensitive to this conflict is seen in its emphasis upon the blockade, not as a means of starvation but as a means of withholding from the enemy foodstuffs which are convertible into munitions. This is an important moral distinction even though it makes more difference to British and American consciences than to German stomachs.

This fourth position seems to me to avoid the self-deceptions which are the danger that goes with the first, the fatalism which is characteristic of the second, and unlike the third it is a position that can control the choices of those who remain in public life in the times when choices are hardest.[7]

[7]This analysis parallels in part the controversies concerning the Orders of creation and preservation (*Ordnungen*)

Many of the issues already discussed will be clarified if we consider the claims of pacifism as the Christian way of life in times of social conflict. By pacifism I shall mean the absolute rejection of all violence that has as its immediate objective the taking of human life. This is far short of Tolstoyan absolutism, but it is the only kind of pacifism that is persuasive to many modern Christians. As we find pacifism in our midst, it usually involves three different convictions:

1. That violence of the type described is under all circumstances the greatest evil and is therefore to be renounced in advance.

2. That such violence is always self-defeating in its consequences. ("Satan cannot cast out Satan.")

3. That there is a positive Christian strategy of love available for all situations, and if at any time we do

---

in Continental theology. The Orders are the permanent structures of social life, such as the state or the family, which are so necessary to our existence that they are regarded as the result of God's creative work. There are at least three ways of dealing with the Orders. One is to deny that they have any bearing on our knowledge of God's will. A second is to identify the orders with existing institutions, especially with existing nations. This is a convenient rationalization of the National Socialist claims for the nation. A third is to emphasize the fact that the present form of the Orders is the result of sin and that hence all existing institutions should be dealt with critically. This third position corresponds roughly with the fourth position in my analysis. It is set forth in Brunner's *The Divine Imperative,* one of the greatest books on Christian ethics. Brunner is inclined to take a too static view of the Orders, for although the Orders as they stand are infected by sin the whole human situation is so controlled by sin that radical reconstruction of society seems out of the question. But there are always two Brunners in every book and he corrects this static emphasis in another side of his thought.

not see what that strategy is, in the light of the other two convictions, it is for us to renounce violence and wait, taking upon ourselves as far as possible the immediate consequences of non-violence and leaving the more remote consequences to God.

These three convictions do not necessarily go together. It is possible to believe the first without accepting either of the others as representing universal truths. On the other hand, most pacifists will be so sure in all situations that the way of violence is self-defeating that they will have confirmation for their absolute from their interpretation of events. If they cannot point to a positive strategy that will solve the problem on the political level, they may at least concentrate on the task of healing or of preserving a spirit and a witness that will be needed when the emergency is over.

Pacifism, as I have described it, has some claim to be regarded as in a special way a Christian point of view. It is an extension of aspects of the teaching of Jesus and rests in part on a generalization from Jesus' own dealing with evil. It depends for its influence, at least in the Western world, on Christian moral sensitivity. In the hardest places it would have no message of hope if it were not for the Christian teaching concerning the cross and if it were not for faith in the God of love as the Lord of history. Christians who are not pacifists can agree with the pacifist that all use of violence against persons is desperately evil. With the pacifist they should be ready to translate the destruction of war into the personal fate of millions of men, women and children. With the pacifist they should put the burden of proof on any one who says: "Now is the time for making an exception to all that we have taught concerning human relations; now is the time (as Bergson suggests that nations do in time of war) to say with Macbeth's witches: 'Fair is foul, and foul is fair.' " The Christian who is not a pacifist can hardly concede to the state the right to use him in the perpetration of any cruel or treacherous deed that the exigencies of war may suggest to callous military minds. The difficulty of drawing the line anywhere when once one is a part of a military machine gives strength to the pacifist case from the Christian point of view. There are occasions when non-pacifist Christians will join pacifist Christians as conscientious objectors against a war which both find unjustified. Moreover, the Christian who is not a pacifist must recognize that the pacifist has chosen one Christian way that all Christians should honor.

What the non-pacifist Christian rightly contends is that pacifism is not a self-sufficient social strategy available at all times to the nation and to those who are responsible for public policy, and that, since Christians have responsibility for public policy, pacifism is not the only decision open to the Christian who seeks to be sensitive and obedient. There are four reasons which drive me against my will to this conclusion.

1. Christian love involves a double imperative. On the one hand it is an imperative against violence; but, also, it makes us responsible for the restraint of evil. In concrete situations we find a conflict between the two sides of the imperative of love, and there is no law carrying its own prescription for application to such situations which can resolve that conflict. We cannot

even use the example of Jesus as one to be imitated because his function was different from that of those responsible for public policy. Moreover, the historical circumstances of his life were not the same as those that we face. The struggle of the Jews against the Roman Empire was a more hopeless struggle than, for example, the attempt of the Chinese to limit the area of Japanese control. I believe also that Jesus was sufficiently influenced by the apocalyptic thinking of his time to be able to concentrate upon the Kingdom of God in absolute terms to the neglect of the immediate political consequences of his choices. This concentration upon the Kingdom in absolute terms enabled Jesus to teach an ethic that would be the norm for every future situation but not a law to be applied mechanically to all concrete problems.

When violence is already in progress and the question at issue is not that of violence or no violence but whether one side is to be able to dictate to the other terms of surrender, then those who are responsible for public policy may be obliged to continue to use force to prevent such a result. This responsibility is clearest when what is involved is not merely a shifting of boundaries with the prospect of continuity of institutions under a new sovereignty, but the kind of political tyranny that now controls Korea and Poland. Such tyranny not only destroys national independence; it stifles the spiritual life of the people, forcing the independent minds into silence and controlling the education of the children in the interests of the dominant race.[8] Not only pac-

[8]Arthur Geiser, Danzig Nazi leader is quoted as saying: "The Pole is the servant of the German and will remain it forever." (*San Francisco Chronicle,* "This World," page 2, September 1, 1940.)

ifists but also most of us have said many times that no nation can win a modern war, that at the most one side can achieve only nominal success. That argument has lulled us into assuming that it is important to limit the area of war or to stop war but not to be much concerned about the military outcome. Recent events have shown that this argument is not always valid. Unless there is continued resistance to Germany those who live under German rule will not regard German success as "nominal."[9] If it is possible to prevent the extension of such a tyranny it may be right to do so even at the cost of violence. Whether or not it is possible depends on the circumstances, and to that question the Christian gospel cannot give the answer. If the pacifist says, "Wait, this tyranny will defeat itself and crumble in time," the answer is that though it may be true that the tyranny will crumble, that very crumbling will depend upon resistance offered to it at some point, resistance from without or from within.

Another form of the restraint of evil for which the case is quite as strong is the action that may be taken, before the stage of overt violence has arisen, to prevent violence. Many American pacifists say that action should have been taken much earlier, in the case of Manchuria or in the case of Ethiopia, and that if that had been done the present war might have been prevented. I realize that such pacifists are not very con-

[9]A manifesto signed by fifty-one of the leading Christian pacifists in America including a large proportion of the most influential voices in the American pulpit in analyzing the possible results of the war speaks only of two possibilities: "the inevitable exhaustion of all concerned and the nominal success of one party or the other." This appears to have been written in May, 1940. (*Fellowship*, June, 1940.)

sistent and that they would be divided in their own minds. Also, they would rightly call attention to the necessity of accompanying such pressure with a bold policy of international economic readjustment. But any pressure brought by a nation against another nation may lead to reprisals which result in war. It may be granted that the system of collective security which was connected with the League of Nations was too closely tied to the attempt of the most privileged nations to preserve the *status quo,* but in the future any form of collective security will involve some risk of violence in the effort to prevent far more widespread violence. If that is true, it seems quite obvious that while absolute pacifism may be a vocation for some individuals it is not a self-sufficient strategy for the nation. To forfeit all chance to develop a system of collective security because it involves some danger of violence is to condemn the human race to the certainty of perpetual war.

Those who are under the imperative of love must often face the simple fact that if they heed only the warning against violence, they may in some cases become responsible for the evil that might have been restrained had they acted in time. They may be responsible for the encouragement of aggression and for the extension of tyranny. They may be responsible for the war that they dared not try to prevent by collective pressure that involved but a marginal risk of war.

2. No nation as a nation can be expected to have the moral discipline to live according to the pacifist faith, paying the price of the cross rather than de-

fending itself or preparing to defend itself. Nations with mixed populations are not able to play the role that may be open to a small Christian group. An acute observer recently remarked to me that there is probably more hate in Czecho-Slovakia without war than in China with war. It is often suggested that the non-violent policy of Denmark may be an illustration of how a nation can be pacifistic. But, while it may be true that when resistance is impossible such a policy is expedient for the nation, Denmark in not resisting became an unwilling instrument of Germany in her attacks upon Norway and upon England. Statesmen in time of national danger have a clear obligation to provide for the defense of their people. Any persons responsible for public policy who fail, for example, to provide for defense against air raids are recreant to their duty unless their people deliberately choose to remain undefended in the light of full knowledge of the facts. The possibility of such a deliberate choice on the part of any people is remote indeed. The pacifist may seek to persuade the people to make that choice, but if he fails he has no right to use any position of political influence he may have to frustrate that will to be prepared for defense.

Professor C. J. Cadoux, a leader of the English pacifists, in his book *Christian Pacifism Re-examined* comes to the conclusion that only a nation that is controlled by the motives of Christian pacifism can adopt a pacifist policy. He believes that the "second best" policy for England today, even from his point of view as a pacifist, is not surrender or the attempt to negotiate with Hitler while he is still able to preserve his conquests but continued resistance. Pacifism remains a necessary vocation for a minority group but this vocation does not consist in bringing pressure on the nation to adopt a policy which, because it is externally non-violent, seems to resemble pacifism but which in this context, in view of the real alternatives open to the nation, would lead to the greater evil. Elton Trueblood has shown that an attitude of this kind has support from the three hundred years of Quaker history.[10]

3. The conviction of most American pacifists that there is always a strategy of non-violence open to those who would take it is more often true than most people are willing to admit, but it is not universally true. Pacifism that seeks to preserve personal integrity and to keep alive influences of mercy in the world which cannot be expected to make an immediate difference in the political situation does not require this conviction, but actually American pacifism does quite largely depend upon it. If a situation does arise in which there is no non-violent way of preventing aggression or tyranny, it would seem that those responsible for short-run consequences are obliged to use military force for that purpose if there is any hope of success. Whether or not there is hope of success cannot be deduced from any absolute ethical principle. If the pacifist turns political analyst and offers advice to the effect that there is no such hope, let him not eke out arguments based upon inadequate evidence with a half-concealed absolute that begs the question. When public opinion is not ready for the pacifist strategy or

[10]See article "The Quaker Way," in *The Atlantic Monthly,* December, 1940.

when that strategy does not fit the objective situation, *some one must act and must take responsibility for short-run consequences as things actually are.* It is too late for a policy based upon choices that might have been made five or ten years before.

I have suggested that there are situations in which the pacifist strategy of non-violence is not available. When violence has reached the stage of air raids, what possible non-violent strategy is available against a thousand raiders four miles high? The most baffling example of such a situation is to be found when it is necessary to deal with a nation which, because of censorship and propaganda, is impervious to moral persuasion. How can we persuade by word, by action, even by suffering, when we cannot get through the spiritual walls built by censorship and propaganda? Even love would seem to be weakness and hypocrisy, and there is always so much evil in the past of the nation that may have a relatively just cause that propaganda can easily misrepresent the motives behind its policy. I do not mean that the people in any great nation are all impervious to persuasion were it possible for them to know the truth. But it is impossible for them to know facts that are available to the outside world. There must be some measure of spiritual continuity, resulting from confrontation by the same facts as well as from common standards and loyalties, between victims and oppressors if such moral pressure is to win the hearts of the latter group. Gandhi's technique of non-violence gains results in dealing with the British government which allows publicity for his every move and which is itself responsive to a large section of public opinion favorable to the cause of India. But one can only imagine how much attention Gandhi's fasts would have if he were in a Nazi concentration camp; his death would be welcomed by his keepers and it would probably be announced that he was shot while trying to escape. Such a strategy of non-violence would have no chance of making an impression upon the people in the oppressing nation if Gandhi were a Czech, a Pole, or a Korean.

4. I do not believe that pacifists, especially in America, face the problem that arises when they themselves do not bear the brunt of the suffering to which their policy of non-violence may contribute. American pacifists talk much about the cross, but the suffering in this situation—I do not say "the cross" because it is mostly involuntary suffering—is not borne by them but by people in China, in London, in the nations of Europe that have lost their freedom. Knowing many pacifists as well as I do, I have no doubt that if there were a way by which they could divert this suffering to themselves they would choose to do so, but there is no such way open to them. When there is no redemptive way of the cross open to Christians in a situation, it is important for them not to disguise their responsibility for the increase of the sufferings of others by the use of words that suggest falsely that they are the ones who suffer.

In this discussion of pacifism I have sought to show only one thing—that pacifism does not provide a short cut to Christian decision in all situations. The role of the pacifist is for the individual and for the minority group and not for the statesman or for those who are responsible for public policy. Let not the pacifist claim to have absolute guidance for the next step when possibilities are so limited that there is no choice save resistance or the encouragement of aggression or tyranny. But let the statesmen and those responsible for public policy never close their minds to the insights of the pacifist. He has no self-sufficient strategy which he can prescribe for them but he can remind them of those aspects of the truth that they are in the greatest danger of forgetting.

Before I leave this discussion of pacifism I want to emphasize the fact that there has developed within the Church—and to some extent outside the Church—an attitude toward war that is far in advance of the attitude of the conventional patriot who identifies the cause of his nation with his religion and yet which is not that of the absolute pacifist. That it has become widespread in the past twenty years leads me to believe that the intensive peace education of those years has left an important deposit even if the external situation shows little evidence of it. The disillusionment about war which has been so pervasive may have led many to a moral indifferentism concerning the issues involved in this war, but there is genuine moral insight in that disillusionment which must not be lost. This attitude toward war of which I speak is not new in history. It was essentially Abraham Lincoln's attitude. There is a lesson for pacifists in the fact that, although almost all of Lincoln's public life on a national scale was devoted to the prosecution of a war, Lincoln is known to us primarily as a man of magnanimity and deep humanity. It was possible for him to participate in war and at the same time to transcend its passions and preserve his integrity as a human being. An attitude that resembles Lincoln's has been crystallized in recent years. I believe that it is the only attitude—other than the position of the pacifist—which has any right in the Christian Church.

Non-pacifist Christians who share this attitude believe that there are occasions on which they must participate in military force but they have no illusions about it. They know, for one thing, that their nation is in part responsible for the situation out of which war has come. They know that war can do no more than check an evil force and that what hope there is of anything good coming out of the conflict depends upon the character of the peace. They know that the peace that followed the last war was a failure and that the minds of their nations must be prepared to prevent a repetition of that failure. They know also that their own nation in the hour of victory will be tempted to misuse the power that victory brings. They are determined to keep alive the world Church and to renew their ties with Christians in the enemy nation as soon as war is over. (In the case of Chinese and Japanese Christians some of these ties have been preserved during the conflict and in Europe indirect contacts are still possible between Christians in belligerent nations through the machinery of the World Council of Churches.) They will be in a position to do this because they realize that the war is a judgment upon all nations for a common sin and not the product of one evil national will.

The best test of this attitude that I am describing is to be found in the capacity of those who claim to share it to retain fellowship with conscientious objectors within the Church. Those who truly represent this attitude are keenly aware of the bitter dilemma that confronts the Christian mind on this issue; they are not surprised to find other Christians who disagree with them in their immediate decision; they welcome the fact that there is a pacifist minority to remind them of Christian demands which they are tempted to forget and to supplement them in the Church so that the message of the Church as a whole may be more Christian. When we are forced by circumstances to make one-sided decisions, the decisions of each of us including those of the pacifist need this kind of correction. The Christian non-pacifist prays that the time may not be long before he can join with the pacifists in the tasks of healing and reconstruction.[11]

My answer to those who accuse the Churches of changing their position about war three times in twenty years—changes which on the surface must be admitted so far as the British Churches and part of the leadership

[11] I refer those who may doubt that this position can hold up under the pressures of war to *The Christian News-Letter* published in England under the editorship of Doctor J. H. Oldham; to the Archbishop of York's *Thoughts in War-Time;* to a series of booklets on the war published in London by the Student Christian Movement Press. This attitude was formulated in the report of The Oxford Conference and in the report of the Conference held at Geneva in July, 1939. The official attitudes of the Churches toward conscientious objectors in this country and in England is a matter of record that points to a real gain.

of the American Churches are concerned—is that it does not do justice to the development of this Christian form of non-pacifism which I have described. This represents a solid result of the work of the peace movements in the Churches. The Christian Churches, where the influence of Christian pacifism has been strongest, have not returned to the simple identification of Christianity with the national cause or to the uncritical "presenting of arms" that we associate with the first World War.

I have tried to show the reasons for the very great difficulty in identifying Christianity with particular social programs and movements. If there is any large measure of truth in what I have said it is necessary for us to envisage a more indirect relationship between Christian teaching and concrete social decisions. I wish that the situation were simpler but I see no way to escape from this conclusion. Christian teaching should be directed primarily to the development of Christian minds that will discipline themselves in obedience. In common worship they should seek to fit themselves to make decisions from a Christian perspective.

The conclusion of this chapter will be an attempt to outline this Christian perspective. The best that we can hope for is that there may develop among us a company of people who will seek honestly to make their concrete social decisions in the light of this perspective. To share this perspective involves a change in the minds of individuals but it is not the same as conversion to an individualistic gospel. Such conversions do not necessarily lead to Christian social insight. As the Madras report says: "Social change will come from individual change only when the content of social change is put within the concept and fact of individual change."[12]

1. First of all, there are the standards by which every social order and every proposal for reform must be tested—such standards as these: justice in the form of equal opportunity for all persons regardless of nationality, race or class; fellowship between persons across all existing barriers; restraints upon arbitrary power and positive protection of freedom of thought and conscience for minorities; the structure of society made favorable for the development of persons of deep moral integrity and religious devotion. A society can be called more or less Christian depending upon its relation to these standards.

2. These standards need to be sharpened at one point especially: they should lead to a great reversal of the habits of nearly every society to control its life for the benefit of the top fraction—perhaps less than a tenth, perhaps as much as a third of the population. The people in our Churches have long had the habit of giving the benefit of the doubt in all great controversial issues to this top fraction. Now they are called upon to give the benefit of the doubt to those who have been most exploited and most insecure. This means concretely that as they see unskilled labor, ten-

[12]*The World Mission of the Church,* page 107. I have discussed this problem more fully in a previous book *Social Salvation,* Chapter 2.

ant farmers, Negroes, migrants, unemployed struggling for the bread and the status that they themselves take for granted, they know that, whatever the faults those groups or their leaders may share with the more privileged, the objectives for which they organize politically and in labor unions are essentially just. In relation to them there has been a bias dictated by the middle-class complacency that is the peculiar temptation of most American Protestants. Christianity cannot give us a short cut to a solution of their problems but it can guide us to change our bias—to give the benefit of the doubt where we have been inclined to deny it. I submit that unless we cultivate the habit of mind that sees the world from the point of view of those who have least privilege we can have no part at all in the mind of Christ.

3. A third aspect of this Christian perspective which I have already suggested in my remarks about repentance is to be found in the Christian teaching concerning human nature. It is of the greatest importance that we have within the orbit of the Church those who, instead of concentrating upon the sins of their opponents or enemies, see first their own sins. This is another reversal of the usual bias, for it is natural to see first the sins of other groups. Those who seek to accomplish this reversal in themselves may not have any simple answer to the question raised by our most perplexing problems but they will be distrustful of rationalizations of policies that harmonize with their own interests. In the midst of conflict of all kinds they will be able to avoid self-righteous fanaticism because they will know too well the failings of their own

hearts. They will be leaven in society that will do much to moderate social conflicts.

4. Those who have accepted the discipline suggested by the aspects of the Christian perspective already presented may know not only the challenge of the Christian religion but also its consolation. The Christian can see the whole of history as the arena of God's activity. This will be the basis of morale. He can know that however dark the age in which he lives the most powerful forces in the world are those that are in line with God's intention. He can also know that when he has done his best there is divine forgiveness for his part in the evil that remains. He can also know that there is an order within the larger order of society and yet not of it, an order of life that has as its structure the Christian Church. To this order he can belong. He can hope to Christianize the Church before it is possible to Christianize the world and all that he can do now, even in times of social frustration, to strengthen the fellowship of the world Church will be the means of keeping alive the forces of redemption through this age into the age that will follow. It is these forces of redemption in which he will put his greatest trust, whatever hard decisions he may make on the political level, and to them he will look for God's new beginning. It is to a consideration of these forces of redemption that we shall turn in the next chapter.

CHAPTER FIVE

THE MOVEMENT OF REDEMPTION

(1) CHRIST

There is a movement in history which is in a distinctive way the carrier of God's redemptive influence. This movement has its roots in the dim past when the religion of Israel showed that it possessed a capacity for development that separated it from other Semitic cults. The clearest figure in the early history of this movement is the figure of Moses, though Moses points to predecessors who are but shadows in the background.

We see that this movement is the carrier of something that is universal when we come upon the prophets. In an earlier chapter I referred to the remarkable story of the prophet Nathan who stands before King David and says to him: "Thou art the man." In this story we have the elements most necessary for the growth of a universal religion. There is God who is above the King. There is the prophet who is free to speak the unwelcome truth to the King in the name of God. There is the common man who is more than a subject of the King and who has rights before God which the King must respect. There is God's concern for justice in human relations. There is the King's own repentance. There is the beginning of the idea of divine forgiveness. A religion that is merely the means of sanctifying the will of the King or the interest of a nation has little chance to develop. As early as a thousand years before Christ we see that there is something more than that in the religion of Israel. The development of this religion through the great prophets from Amos to Second Isaiah is momentous for our knowledge of God and for the growth of the human conscience, more momentous than philosophical speculation or ethical theory.

It is against the background of this development in the Old Testament that we must understand Jesus. He took for granted the higher stages of the Old Testament faith, carried them to fulfillment and made the treasures of that faith available for all humanity. He was himself the inheritor of the tendency toward universalism that we find in Second Isaiah. In his own teaching he carried that tendency farther. After the rejection of Jesus by the Jewish leaders of his generation, the universalism already implicit in Jesus' thought became explicit and absolute in Paul. "There can be neither Jew nor Greek, there can be neither bond nor free, there can be no male and female; for ye are all one in Christ Jesus." (Gal. 3:28.) In those words we reach one of the goals of religion beyond which it is impossible to advance.

Jesus did more than make universal what was already present in the Hebrew faith, though if he had done only that our debt to him would be beyond calculation. He carried farther than his predecessors the idea of God's forgiving love that seeks to save even the lost sheep, and at the same time he sharpened the moral demand that God makes upon man in terms of love and responsibility for those who count for least in the eyes of society. Also, without losing the sense of the importance of the deed, he placed new emphasis upon the motives of men, upon inner clarity. The arguments about the original elements in the teachings of Jesus are usually inconclusive, but it appears to me that these elements that I have mentioned are original in their sharpness. In general it is freshness of emphasis rather than complete novelty in which we must expect to find the originality of Jesus.[1]

Jesus did more than bring to fulfillment the teachings of the Old Testament, more than add to those teachings whatever elements we may discover in the gospels as original. He also embodied the truth about life and the truth about God that his words reveal. Again, it is not that we are to look for new qualities of unselfishness or courage which we find nowhere else. Rather we discover in Jesus a balance of quali-

[1]C. G. Montefiore regards the seeking out of sinners as the original element in the attitude of Jesus: "The Rabbis attached no less value to repentance than Jesus. They sang its praises and its efficacy in a thousand tones. They, too, urged that God cared more for the repentant than for the just who had never yielded to sin. They, too, welcomed the sinner in his repentance. But to *seek out* the sinner, and, instead of avoiding the bad companion, to choose him as your friend in order to work his moral redemption, this was, I fancy, something new in the religious history of Israel." *Some Elements of the Religious Teaching of Jesus,* page 57. Joseph Klausner confirms this judgment in his criticism of Jesus for encouraging moral indifference.

ties which is not only unique but also supreme in its claim upon our reverence. To that we must add the fact that the character of Jesus was tested by the cross. Had he lived for eighty years and died a normal death, he might have been all we know that he was, but we could not be sure that his love for men and his devotion to God would stand the ultimate test.

But the most important thing remains to be said. Jesus, who fulfilled the religious development of more than a thousand years, was the beginning of a new stage in the relations between God and men. His death was not the end but the beginning of his power.

The resurrection of Christ means two things at least. Understood in the most general terms it is a symbol for the fact that Christ has actually triumphed over death in history. But it also refers to a specific event, to the event which initiated the Christian movement. What the real nature of this event was we do not know and probably we shall never know. The evidence that is closest to the event itself is the account of Paul, confirmed by the gospels, of the appearances of Christ to the disciples. But the most important evidence for the resurrection as an event is to be found in the Christian movement based upon it, which links our lives with those of the first disciples. To affirm a resurrection of Christ's physical body from the tomb is in the line of least resistance for the orthodox. To deny the event entirely and affirm the resurrection only as a symbol of a general principle is in the line of least resistance for the religious liberal. I believe that we may remain in closer touch with the realities if we do neither, but rather affirm that all that we know of the event is that visions of Christ after his death were the means by which the disciples became assured of what was essentially true—*the continuing presence of God as the Living Christ and as the Spirit in the work that Jesus had begun.* As Johannes Weiss says: "Conceived as visions, the events of the first Easter may lose something of their apologetic value *for us;* but then they scarcely took place for our benefit, but rather in the interest of those immediately concerned. For them, the vision sufficed, and produced a certainty of conviction which made them inspired missionaries and martyrs."[2]

Paul helps us to some extent in his classifying of the appearances to the disciples together with the appearance of Christ to himself. The validity of the latter appearance does not depend upon the empty tomb; nor does it depend upon the accuracy of the details of Paul's vision on the road to Damascus. It seems to be a fact to which our rationalistic habits of mind should not blind us that great moments in the history of the human spirit often take such forms. Even Socrates, the father of rational philosophy, was himself controlled in his mission by the oracle of Delphi and by the "dæmon" that accompanied him. We, with our inhibitions, may not have such experiences, but it is not for us to discredit the truth of which they were the vehicle.[3] Instead of saying that the Christian movement is discredited by the illusory

[2]*History of Primitive Christianity,* Volume I, page 29.

[3]I owe the realization of the significance of this side of Socrates to Bergson's discussion in *The Two Sources of Morality and Religion,* page 53.

elements in the visions on which it was founded, it would be sounder to say that the visions on which it was founded proved to be the means by which the earliest Christians became convinced of a truth which has been tested by the continued power of Christ over the minds and consciences of men.

The most important area of controversy concerning Jesus in contemporary thought is the controversy about the relative importance of the teachings and personality of the Jesus of history and the Christ of faith. This controversy in its present form presupposes two convictions about the Jesus of history which were not necessarily presupposed in the nineteenth century when advanced thought under Hegelian influence was preoccupied with the universal Christ. These two convictions are, first, that there is no doubt about the actual existence of Jesus and, second, that the fact that Jesus was an historical character is essential, for it is in that fact that we find God active in human history. It is the historical fact of the incarnation that is usually assumed even when the teachings and personal qualities of the incarnate one are not emphasized. Without this degree of historicity there would be no basis for faith in the incarnation, the cross, the resurrection as redeeming acts of God. But that faith often goes with an astonishing neglect of the Jesus of history on the part of those who make absolute claims for his divine mission. Karl Barth, whose claims for the revelation of God in Christ are absolute in the most unqualified sense, is also author of what may be the most disparaging sentence written by any contemporary theologian about the Jesus of history: "Jesus Christ in fact is also the Rabbi of Nazareth, historically so difficult to get information about, and when it is got, one whose activity is so easily a little commonplace alongside more than one other founder of a religion and even alongside many later representatives of his own religion."[4] Paul Tillich, who claims that we find in Christ the center of history and the criterion by which to test all our knowledge of God, is also inclined to suggest that we do not need to depend upon the Jesus of history. How can we explain this tendency to make absolute claims for the divine work of Christ and yet to neglect his actual teachings and personality?

There are at least five reasons for this tendency, which I shall summarize: 1. *Historical scepticism about the gospels.* The existence of Jesus is not questioned by responsible scholars, but the outline of his life has been torn apart by Form Criticism with its analysis of the gospel material into small units which were preserved because they were useful in the preaching of the early Christian community. The tendency has been to emphasize the work of the Christian community in the development of the gospels. Perhaps more important is the general effect produced by the variety of the interpretations of Jesus which have the support of scholars. These interpretations seem to cancel each other, leaving little assured knowledge concerning the Jesus of history. It is to avoid the necessity of building faith upon such uncertainties that many of our contemporaries turn their attention to the Christ of dogma or to the Christ of the experience of the Church.

[4] *The Doctrine of the Word of God,* page 188.

2. *The emphasis upon the Pauline interpretation of Christ as the essence of Christianity.* Preoccupation with the Pauline doctrine of redemption has seemed to furnish a conception of Christianity for which the Jesus of history is relatively unimportant. Martin Dibelius says in describing the result of much recent research into the origins of Christianity: "The *fact* that Jesus was a man is decisive for faith; *how* this earthly life was lived seems to be of no importance."[5]

3. This emphasis upon Paul's interpretation of Christ has been much strengthened by *disillusionment concerning the application of the ethical teachings of Jesus.* The center of Christianity is naturally shifted to the gospel of forgiveness for those who find that they do not and cannot live by the law of love. This is very well expressed in a letter recently received from a young English theologian. After discussing the problem created by the war he says: "Hence, the Sermon on the Mount must be interpreted theologically or rather Christologically, and apart from this kind of interpretation, it is a counsel of despair. As Niebuhr would say, it is not a 'simple possibility' for us . . . on the contrary, it sets up (as St. Matthew rightly sees) a New Law, which condemns all our efforts to fulfill it. . . . We must begin with the recognition that Christ is our despair, until he becomes our hope."

Two rather different reasons can be mentioned which may well accompany considerable emphasis upon the Jesus of history, but which suggest the inadequacy of a type of Christianity for which the Jesus of history is in an exclusive way the center. 4. *The*

[5]*Gospel Criticism and Christology,* page 12.

need of fresh guidance in our situation which is different from the situation that Jesus faced. This may lead to an emphasis on the Church or on the living spirit of Christ who shall lead us into all truth. 5. *The desire for a broader base for Christianity than the few months or years of the public life of Jesus.* Walter Horton suggests that to stress only the Jesus of history is not unlike the standing of a pyramid on its apex. We can base Christian faith upon the whole range of the movement of redemption–including the preparation for Christ in the Old Testament and the impact of Christ upon his followers in the Church.

I believe that this tendency to neglect the Jesus of history threatens Christianity with a great perversion. Perhaps, so long as this generation remembers as much about Jesus as it does, we shall not see this perversion at its worst for some time to come. The minds of most of those who now represent the tendency to neglect the Jesus of history were formed in large part by the gospels. They naturally read into the Christ of their faith the content of the teachings and personality of Jesus. But let another generation arise that is brought up from the beginning on this theology that neglects Jesus and we may expect to find Christianity a cult of salvation which has forgotten that, though salvation may not be earned by works, the most important test of its presence is ethical. It is always a bad day for Christianity when preoccupation with either sacramental or evangelical short cuts to the religious goal prevents Christians from hearing the words: "Inasmuch as ye did it not . . ."

I emphasize the importance of the Jesus of history for the following reasons:

1. The scepticism about the Jesus of history is exaggerated. We may admit that the order of events in the gospels is not to be relied on; we may admit that the gospels were the products of the preaching of the early Christian community and not the work of critical historians; but at least we can still affirm that there comes to us through the gospels a coherent body of teaching and many glimpses of Jesus in action which are consistent with that teaching. In his authoritative study of a century of investigation of the gospels, Professor C. C. McCown comes to this conclusion: "Yet there is enough of the story remaining to picture a person whose personal character and fundamental ideas are clearly established." Professor McCown, himself trained by those who have done most in this country to emphasize the part of the early Christian community in the development of the materials in the gospels, turns this emphasis into a sound reason for approaching the gospels with more confidence than scepticism.[6]

The one-sided interpretations of the teachings of Jesus represented by such men as Schweitzer and Harnack do perhaps cancel each other, but they leave the possibility of a more balanced interpretation which

[6]"The Synoptic materials took shape and the Gospels were written during the first Christian generation, or before the eyewitnesses of Jesus' life had all passed away. It is safe to say that the Gospel of John would have been impossible in Palestine or Syria in 65 A.D. The unforgettable impression which Jesus had made upon his friends, the indescribable significance of his life and words in their theories of the salvation which he had wrought for them, gave accounts of his life a value that led to exaggeration and overemphasis on some features in the earlier years, but would not allow serious falsification and distortion such as the Fourth Gospel exhibits." *The Search for the Real Jesus,* page 206.

recognizes that Jesus belonged to the first century and not to the nineteenth, that he shared the apocalyptic expectation which was characteristic of the best piety among his Jewish contemporaries and yet he was not so obsessed by it that his teaching can be understood from that perspective alone.

Most suggestive of the trustworthiness of the gospels as sources for the teaching and the personality of Jesus is the coherence of the teaching and the glimpses of him in action that we find in all the sources into which the gospels can be analyzed. Professor C. H. Dodd in his *History and the Gospel* has shown in detail how far this is true in the case of many of the aspects of Jesus' character and teachings. I shall give one illustration of this coherence of the gospels: the attitude of Jesus toward social outcasts. One sees this in the Markan narratives of the call of Levi (Mark 2:14) and of the feast with publicans and sinners (Mark 2:15–17); in the Lukan narratives concerning the woman in Simon's house (Luke 7:36–38) and of Zacchæus (Luke 19:2–10); in the Lukan parable of the Pharisee and the Publican (Luke 18:10–14); in the parable of the lost sheep that is common to Matthew and Luke (Luke 15:4–7 and Matthew 18:12–13); in the saying peculiar to Matthew to the effect that "the publicans and harlots enter the Kingdom of God before you" (Matthew 21:32). Also the story of the woman taken in adultery, which is found in the Gospel of John (John 7:53–8:11) and which is in some manuscripts of Luke, fits perfectly the picture of Jesus which we find in these passages. If it is possible to know anything about an ancient historical figure it is possible to know that Jesus was one whose love broke through the prejudices of His society to those who were most despised.[7]

We may not know enough to write a biography of Jesus, but we know enough about him to draw his portrait. Just as we see him with outcasts we see him also with children; we see him healing—not to provide a sign as the Fourth Gospel would have us think, but because of his natural response to human need; we see him as he speaks boldly in the synagogue at Nazareth, touching to the quick the racial prejudice of his hearers and expressing his concern for the concrete forms of human suffering in this world to which no purely apocalyptic interpretation of his mission can do justice; we see him as with the wisdom of serpents he outwits his captious critics; we see him as he lashes out against the sins of the respectable and the strong; we see him as he wrestles with the suggestion of his disciples that he take the easy road rather than the road that will lead to the cross; we see him in Gethsemane as he commits himself to God when the road nears its end; we see him as he goes to his death with dignity and with love, embodying in his own person the best attested of all his sayings: "He that saveth his life shall lose it; and he that loseth his life for my sake and the gospel's shall save it."

2. The tendency to neglect the Jesus of history cannot really be reconciled with the thought of the New Testament as a whole. It is quite true that if one approaches the New Testament with a mind dominated

[7]I am following here Professor Dodd's analysis on pages 92–93.

by the dogmatic scheme into which Protestant theology has fitted the first half of the epistle to the Romans, the importance of the teachings and personality of Jesus seems small indeed. But if one approaches Paul through First Corinthians, the emphasis to which one comes is quite different. It is true that Paul does not often quote Jesus and that he refers to few events in his life. But Paul was saturated with what he had learned of the mind and spirit of Jesus, so much so that he could express that mind and spirit without direct quotation. Doctor Frank Porter in the first chapter of *The Mind of Christ in Paul* seems to me to provide irrefutable evidence of the continuity between Paul and Jesus. He refers, for example, to the thirteenth chapter of First Corinthians in this way: "The centre of the chapter, the characterization of love itself (verses 4–7), constitutes a picture of Jesus himself, and is derived from him. It has no other historical explanation. So that although Christ is not mentioned in the chapter, it is one of Paul's greatest testimonies to the personality of Jesus, to that which Paul knew him to be. It is a portrait of the character of Jesus drawn by one whom this chapter itself proves to have been a great artist; great, too, in his appreciation of the divine beauty and truth of the mind he is depicting."[8]

Christ for Paul was no *deus ex machina* who might have been any one so far as his actual teachings and personality are concerned, whose only importance was that through him God was able to perform certain acts of redemption; Christ was also a spirit who had the

[8]Page 24.

marks of Jesus of Nazareth. The fruits of his spirit were: "love, joy, peace, long-suffering, kindness, goodness, faithfulness, meekness, self-control." When Paul says: "Have this mind in you, which was also in Christ Jesus," the most important element in that mind is shown by the fact that Christ had "emptied himself, taking the form of a servant." Paul here is referring to the belief that the pre-existent Christ became incarnate. Is it an accident that those words also apply to the character of the Jesus of history, that they fit so well Jesus' own saying: "If any man would be first, he shall be last of all, and servant of all" (Mark 9:35)?

John may almost lose the human Jesus in his conception of the incarnate Logos walking the earth in Palestine but not quite. He had clearly received the impression of one of whom it was fitting to think that he consorted with Samaritans and that he would wash the feet of his disciples. During the days of his ministry it was possible to perceive his glory and to realize that he was full of grace and truth. Given that initial experience of Jesus, it was possible on the basis of later events to see the Jesus of history overshadowed by the glory of the pre-existing and the living Lord, but would that later development have been possible without the initial experience of Jesus as one who was in fact "full of grace and truth"? I believe not. One may also wonder whether, if the words and example of Jesus of Nazareth had not been in the background, the author of the first epistle of John would have preserved in so central a way the ethical emphasis that we find in the words: "If a man say 'I love God' and hateth his brother, he is a liar: for he that loveth not his brother whom he hath seen, cannot love God whom he hath not seen."

3. No theology about Christ can supersede the essential wisdom of the teachings of Jesus. Jesus was no "liberal moralist" but neither was he an apocalyptic fanatic. His apocalyptic perspective enabled him to concentrate on the moral absolute rather than on next steps for the Jews in Palestine in the first century. As it was, he spoke of the conditions of entrance into the Kingdom of God, which is the goal for human living in every century. He emphasized both the fatherhood of God and the sovereignty of God, both the forgiving love of God and the judgment of God. He saw most clearly the structure of life—the necessity of the commitment that involves the putting off of the narrow self, the demand that we become real and single-minded, the importance of the humble and receptive spirit. It is significant that just as theologians are inclined to neglect the teachings of Jesus, others who are not theologians are rediscovering them because of their psychological soundness.

The teachings of Jesus do not take the place of theology, but they are an extremely important test of theological systems. When the theologian stresses the complete otherness of God who is completely beyond all human analogy he needs to hear Jesus say: "If ye then, being evil, know how to give good gifts unto your children, how much more shall your Father which is in heaven give good things to them that ask him?" (Matthew 7:11). When theologians are tempted to proclaim one-sided views of human nature it is good for them to hear Jesus speak of the evil in man and of the extent to which sin is in the line of least resistance: "For narrow is the gate . . ." But it is also important for them to notice the confidence with which Jesus deals with people, with children who are not yet spoiled by hypocrisy and with all who know that they are sinners. Jesus' story of the Pharisee and the Publican has much in common with the theology of *sola gratia* with its warning against self-righteousness, but it is on a level which is profounder than the theological formulation which invariably becomes more one-sided than the realities of life.

Perhaps the most important contribution of the teachings of Jesus is that they never allow us to escape the ethical demands of God or to forget how central is the love that does not turn away from human need. Just as the theologian who likes to recite his formulas concerning salvation by grace needs to be reminded that Jesus used as his test of discipleship responsiveness to human need, so the Church needs to have the words of Jesus sound forth to test every sacred institution: "the Sabbath was made for man and not man for the Sabbath."

4. The cross and the resurrection gain part of their meaning from the context of the life and personality of Jesus. Not any victim could have been made by divine fiat the means of redemption. Because in the death of Christ we have a clear contrast between divine love and the callousness and cruelty of men, the cross can evoke the best in us. Even for Anselm's doctrine of the cross the character of the human victim was of first importance. Moreover, the cross comes to mean

to us all that we know of Jesus, for in that event his personality is concentrated. The resurrection is the triumph of Jesus and all that he represents. It is the triumph of the love that we find not only on Calvary, but in the whole of the life of Jesus. It is the triumph of faith in God that has no props in external fortune. These events on which theologians concentrate who neglect the Jesus of history would actually become far less significant for their theology if it were not for what we know of the man of Nazareth. Christian piety may have been centered in the death and resurrection of Jesus, but I hazard the opinion that if men knew nothing of the gospel record they would not be captured by any teaching about those events. It is no accident that men such as St. Francis or John Woolman or Kagawa, who seem to embody something of the spirit of the Jesus of the gospels, have been regarded as Christians in a special way by most of us.

5. My final reason for insisting on the central importance of the Jesus of history is that without him we have no norm in testing the many experiences of the contemporary Christ to which men lay claim. I do not mean that Jesus is to be used in a literal and legalistic fashion as the norm for our Christian living, but that there must be in any way of life that is called Christian continuity with his spirit. Without reference to the norm in the gospels it is far too easy for us to imagine a Christ in our own image. Though New Testament scholars and theologians have been quite successful in reading their own ideals and assumptions into the Jesus of the gospels, that process tends to be self-correcting. Doctor John Mackay has said that in conventional religion in South America one hears

little of Christ except as "infant" and as "victim" and that the loss of all the content of the life and teachings of Jesus is a source of great impoverishment. The "infant" at Christmas and the "victim" on Good Friday and the risen Lord of Easter may easily become a part of the sanction of whatever we may seek to preserve in the Church or in the nation. But the Christ who says: "Love your enemies"; "Beware of covetousness"; "Ye cannot serve God and mammon"; the Christ who overturns the tables of the moneychangers; the Christ who excoriates the proud and self-righteous—that Christ is always needed to disturb what we seek to preserve in the Church and in the nation.

While it is important to emphasize the contribution of the Jesus of history to Christianity, it is well to recognize the truth in the protest that we should not limit the basis of Christianity to the few months or years of the public ministry of Jesus. What I am seeking to stress in this chapter is the continuity of the movement of redemption. Both the Old Testament preparation and the impact of Christ upon his followers in the Church belong to this movement. The Jesus of history is the center, but the center is not everything nor would all else be meaningless without it. Rather the center would seem to be a precarious light if it were separated from the movement as a whole. The one thing that would give me greatest reason to raise questions concerning the divine origin of this movement would be for it to have ended at any time as a creative force, leaving humanity oriented entirely toward one segment of the history of the past.

It is an interesting fact that no American thinker has written an influential book on Christology or on the work of Christ in several decades. There have been chapters on those subjects, as for example in Walter Horton's *Realistic Theology,* but more characteristic has been the publication of books on theology which make only a passing mention of such problems. On the other hand nearly every British religious thinker at some time writes a book on one or the other of those subjects. There is something about the conventional discussion of Christology that seems unreal to many of us in America.

I suggest that one way of saying much of what has been central in Christological doctrine is to affirm what I have here affirmed, that Christ is in fact the center of a movement through which God has been at work most distinctively for human redemption. The consciousness of Jesus was that of a human individual. There are no qualifications to be made concerning that and no additions to be made to it on the same level. All speculations about the impersonal humanity of Christ are among the worst examples of deductive theology in trouble; but the human personality of Jesus is our clearest revelation of God's intention for men and the life and death and resurrection of Jesus were the center of that divine activity which is most significant for human living. Without endorsing all that John Macmurray has to say about Jesus, these words of his seem to me to say the most important thing: "Thus Jesus marks the point in history at which it becomes possible for man to adopt consciously as his own purpose the purpose which is already inherent in his nature"[9]—what Macmurray calls elsewhere "the intention of God."

[9] *The Clue to History,* page 55.

If we are to relate a statement such as this to the ancient Christological controversies it seems to me that it resembles most closely one of the convictions of the theologians of Antioch (from the third to the fifth century)—that the union between Jesus and God was a union of will. This can be affirmed without saying that the center of the consciousness of Jesus was identical with the center of the consciousness of the eternal Logos or Son of God; rather we have to do with unity of will or purpose between a human person who was separate in existence and God. God drew this human will to Himself by the same means by which He draws others to Himself, but the influences which played upon the personality of Jesus—his Hebrew background and the persons and events of his immediate environment—made him fit to be the founder of the new religion which released for all humanity the treasures of the old and made him the center of the whole movement of redemption that I have described. The uniqueness of his personal qualities, or the perfection of his humanity, is just as real as we find it to be in history, but it cannot be made more real by doctrines of his nature which set him apart from man altogether. His uniqueness is perhaps most apparent when we take in connection with his human qualities the function which has been his in history. There may be others who in their spheres of life—perhaps in the home circle—approximate the perfection of Christ, but usually they depend upon him directly or indirectly and there are no others who can take his place as the center of the movement of redemption.

There are at least two ways in which we can express the truth in the historic faith in Christ as savior. The first is to point to the direct influence of Christ upon us. This is not limited to the influence of his sufferings upon us, but the death of Christ is the natural climax of his life and it is that which tests to the uttermost all that comes to us through his life and teachings. The moral influence theory of the atonement was cast in these terms. But, as Walter Horton says, that theory has usually been thought of too individualistically and has not done justice to the fact that there has been a change in the current of objective historical forces.[10] So the second way of thinking of Christ as the savior is to see in His life and death the beginning of a new environment for humanity. Because of what Christ did, the world is a radically different place in the sense that the influences and stimuli that surround the soul from birth are radically different. This does not mean that the secular order is necessarily better, but that within the world there is another order which is never entirely controlled by the secular order, an order which is what it is because of the work of Christ.

There are many reasons for criticizing the theology of Schleiermacher, who is usually regarded as the father of liberal Christian thought, but his conception of the redemptive work of Christ seems to me to be of

[10]Walter Horton's treatment of the work of Christ in Chapter Four of *Realistic Theology* is one of the best contemporary discussions of the problem. Since writing that chapter, in a series of Earl Lectures at Pacific School of Religion, Professor Horton has developed his thought along lines suggested by Gustaf Aulén's *Christus Victor*. He seems to think of a cosmic result achieved once for all by Christ's death. In this development I find it difficult to follow him.

permanent value. There are two elements in that conception to which I desire to call attention. The first is the recognition that "the original activity of the Redeemer is best considered as a pervasive influence." This influence, Schleiermacher goes on to say, "is received by its object in virtue of the free movement with which he turns himself to its attraction, just as we ascribe attractive power to every one to whose educational influence we gladly submit ourselves."[11] The effect of Christ's work is to be thought of in terms of persuasion. But this persuasion is mediated, as Schleiermacher says, by the Church. It is through membership in the Christian fellowship that we are influenced by Christ. One should add that, in so far as the spiritual climate in a community has been moulded by Christianity, we find Christ mediated in at least a dim way by persons and movements outside the Church. As John Baillie says: "In these Western lands the Christian gospel has been so long proclaimed that it has not only reached every ear, but left some mark on every heart." And then he asks: "There are many who live as if Christ had never come, but are there any who do so with complete peace of mind?"[12] That those words are less applicable than they were a few years ago is only too obvious, but they do point to a characteristic of what was once Christendom which has not yet been erased. That it will be revived and not erased—whatever may be the events of the next decade—we can be confident, for the work of Christ is uniquely the work of God.

[11] *The Christian Faith,* page 427.
[12] *Our Knowledge of God,* pages 8, 9.

(2) THE CHURCH

Can we believe that this movement of redemption which we find recorded in the Bible and embodied in Christ has been continued? Is it a contemporary fact? It seems to me that the answer to that question depends upon our attitude toward the Christian Church.

There have been those who have believed that the movement of redemption has, in modern times, so pervaded the whole of society that it is the general development of world community or the struggles for social justice on the part of the disinherited to which we are to look for the contemporary redemptive activity of God. Those who have shared this emphasis have had good reason recently to become disillusioned. The trend toward world community on the political or the cultural level has been tragically blocked and the only strand of world community that shows any signs of holding is the Christian Church. The movements of the exploited have been a necessary stimulus and scourge for society and not least for the Church, but they have in most cases failed to organize society, and in the one instance where they have done so, they are suspected of being as much corrupted by power as their predecessors. Given a Christian Church which cuts across class lines and which preserves a basis for criticism of the new centers of power as well as of the old, and there is much hope that secular radical movements can provide part of the drive necessary for the achievement of more equal justice. But without the influence of such a Church there will be little protection against civil war or tyranny. As a bond between persons that moderates class conflict, and as a critic of all centers of power the Church has an indispensable function.

Those who have offered these substitutes for the Church as the modern form of the movement of redemption have had a rather superficial conception of human needs and aspirations. The problem of man is not primarily an economic or political problem. It is finally the problem of finding meaning for his life in the face of sin and suffering and death. If Christianity be true and if God be real it is obvious that there is no solution of the human problem short of man's confronting of God as known in Christ. Outside of the orbit of the Church it is unlikely that many men will so confront God. Their lives will be touched by God in countless ways, but they will not know it.

Within the past few years there has developed a new attitude toward the Church among Protestants. Many of them have rediscovered the Church as the transmitter of the Christian tradition, as the fellowship which they need for their own growth in the Christian life, as a social force that can stand more effectively than any other social force against the power of the state, as the one bond of unity between people of every race, nation and class that can be expected to weather the present storms. I believe that they are right. But I recognize that there are still many liberal Christians who regard this emphasis upon the Church as one more illusion, as one more crutch. I recognize also that most American intellectuals think of the Church as a museum of antiquities which were once impressive or as a congeries of rather ineffective and competing institutions which do little more than give a touch of spirituality to the comfortable middle classes. It is indeed baffling to move from the circles in which the Church is regarded as the world's greatest hope, even though it is criticized with a large measure of objectivity, to those circles in which the Church is ignored as a mere survival. Some one is badly mistaken!

The right perspective from which to view the Church is suggested by some words of Canon Cockin of St. Paul's Cathedral. Recently he wrote: "I believe the Christian Church to be the one hope of salvation for the individual and the community; and I regard it at the moment as itself one of the greatest obstacles to the achievement of its own true aim."[13] In other words it is necessary to do two things at the same time —to make the great affirmations concerning the claims and contribution of the Church and to recognize with the utmost frankness the sins and failures of the Church which cripple its work. We have an early example of this double attitude toward the Church in the apostle Paul. He delivers the most shattering indictment of the particular Church at Corinth to which he writes and at the same time says that it is the Body of Christ. What a shocking thing to write to the members of the Body of Christ: "I praise you not, that ye come together not for the better but for the worse" (1 Cor. 11:17).

No one is more keenly aware of the black strands in the history of the Church or the existing obstacles to its effectiveness as the representative of Christ than

[13]F. A. Cockin, *What Does "A" Do Next?*, page 57.

those who believe in the Church. They do not forget that the Church has been a tyrant and persecutor, that it has sanctified many a secular tyranny and put a premium on orthodoxy at the expense of intellectual honesty. They do not forget that the Church has frequently capitulated to nationalism and that it has found almost every war just—and on both sides. They do not forget that many a war has been turned into a holy war and that the latest example of that is to be found in the attitude of a large part of the Roman Church to the cause of General Franco. They do not forget that the Church has more often than not thrown its weight to the side of the classes in society which have had most privilege and power, and that it is not without reason that the Church has come to be regarded by the masses of mankind in many countries as the enemy of their aspirations. They do not forget that there has been and that there is a vast amount of drabness, pettiness, spiritual mediocrity in the Church, that the Church is far too much like the world, that its divisions reflect this human weakness of the Church more than they do devotion to great convictions, that Churches trust far too much to wealth and prestige, to efficient machinery and expensive eloquence. Continue the indictment as long as you want; add even blacker pages to it and you will not go beyond what those who today believe in the Church are ready to admit.

Before I consider the reasons for believing in the Church in spite of all that can be said against it, I shall pause to explain what I mean when I use the word "Church." I shall use it to refer to the institutions which we call "Churches." There is a sense in which the Church is prior to the Churches, but in so far as the Church in that more ideal and universal sense exists as a functioning reality in our midst it is embodied in the Churches. The true Church of Christ is not coterminous with the Churches. It includes many who are outside the Churches and it excludes many who are in the Churches. But it is to the Churches that we must look for the concentration of the redemptive activity of God in the world. It is important that, as we think of the Churches, we see them against the background of that which unites them rather than as independent local units. The local units are Churches in so far as they point beyond themselves to the Bible, to Christ, to the universal Church, to the Kingdom of God.

This brings me to the most fundamental reason for confidence in what the Church can become in spite of the frankest admission of its failures and sins. It is the fact that when the Church is most true to itself it points beyond itself to that which judges it. This is a Protestant position, but it seems to me to be the most important permanent element in Protestantism. A nation, a political movement may without self-contradiction absolutize itself. But the Church must constantly stand in the presence of God. Loyalty to the Church does not mean accepting it as it is or covering up its faults. Loyalty to the Church means calling the Church back to the sources of its correction and renewal. There is no Church that is so corrupt that it does not cause words to be said every Sunday which condemn it as soon as they are understood. Often in spite of itself, the Church confronts people with Christ, opens to them the Bible. It may make Christ over into its own image, but Christ will in time shatter that image. Periodically, the Church is reformed by a combination of the scourge of external circumstances and by the Spirit of God that is within it.

All through the centuries the Church has steadily done three things. It has helped countless people to relate themselves to God, teaching them the truth about God revealed in Christ, bringing to them a sense of the meaning of their lives, mediating to them the divine forgiveness, giving to them hope in the hardest places of life. The gospel has been too big for the Church to hide. Also, the Church has done a vast amount to tame and to refine the human race, to preserve standards which were recognized even when they were not obeyed, to develop a common mind which was controlled in part by Christian insights. But most important of all, the Church has always nourished minorities which have more fully represented the mind of Christ. There have always been saints, mostly uncanonized, who have kept alive the vision of God and the understanding of man's true nature and possibilities. These minorities have sometimes been in cloisters. They have often been found among the revolutionary sects which the established Church of the time rejected, but which would never have existed apart from the background of the Church. These minorities have also been leaven within the Church, and have been represented among its thinkers and ecclesiastical leaders. (This is remarkably true of the contemporary Church.) We see within the life of the Church a stream of true Christian devotion which has never stopped. In good times and in bad it has been present, exercising an influence all out of proportion to the numbers involved. There is a cumulative aspect of this minority movement within the Church because we today are the heirs of all the prophets and saints. For our own inspiration and guidance we can choose the best from every century.

A very significant reason for faith in the Church is to be found in the trends within the contemporary Church which seem to indicate that we are living in a period of its reformation. I have said that periodically the Church is reformed by the scourge of external circumstance and by the Spirit of God that is within it. We can see both factors at work today. The scourge of external circumstance is creating situations which suggest to many people the defeat of the Church, the restricting of its influence. I think that we must realize that the prestige and power of the Church in the past have been very much inflated. Our ancestors were in many situations converted by force and, until very recent times, the power of the state has bolstered up the institution of the Church. Today the Church must depend upon the adequacy of the Christian religion to meet the needs of men and upon the responsiveness of the world to the truth. No longer is baptism required of holders of public office in many nations. No longer are priests in alliance with the rulers of the state. No longer, except in a few marginal situations, does the state persecute the enemies of the Church —we may be thankful for that. There are still state Churches, but it is true of many of them that they have uneasy consciences about being national Churches. On the mission field the Churches regard the support that they have had from the diplomacy and gunboats of the great powers as an embarrassment. From the external point of view the Church has had many defeats, defeats which may for the moment limit its influence, but which in most cases will purge it and prepare the way for the coming of a Church that is more Christian.

Against this background of external testing and sometimes of institutional defeat there are at least five tendencies within the life of the Church which suggest that we are living in a period of its reformation.

1. The Church in our time has had to endure opposition and often persecution such as has not been known since the days of Constantine. As a result we are able to say that there is iron within the Church, that there are everywhere significant minorities which will become the nucleus of a Church that has been purged and kindled with new flame.

Doubtless if American Protestants a few years ago had chosen the Church that seemed most hopeless, they would have chosen the Russian Orthodox Church. They should have known that there was a strain of mystical devotion in that Church even when it was at its worst, but it took the revolution to reveal that out of that Church there could come a remnant that would be a light for all Christendom. Revolution and exile have freed the best in that Church from its corrupting alliance with an oppressive state and now there have emerged groups of Russian Orthodox Christians who represent profound theological insights and a prophetic attitude toward civilization. The center of these exiles has been Paris. Their influence has been felt through the writings of such men as Nicholas Berdyaev, than whom there is no more fruitful Christian thinker; through their activity in the ecumenical movement and in the Student Christian Movement. These Christians are not counter-revolutionaries who seek to bring back the old Russia.[14] They regard the revolution as a judgment upon the old order that had to come and they wait for the day when Russia will again receive the gospel.

In Germany, as it is well known, there was in the Church a more stubborn open opposition to the government than in any other major institution. This opposition was limited to a few issues which affected the life of the Church itself. It was directed against the attempt of the government to regiment the Church, even to force upon the Church an anti-Semitic policy in relation to its own clergy who have Jewish blood. It was also a protest against the public support of overt paganism. It was not direct opposition to the dictatorship as such or to the nation's foreign policy. We are not to look for pacifism in time of war from this opposition, for the backbone of it is socially conservative and it has strong support in the army.

I say these things because the real significance of the opposition within the German Churches to official

[14]Berdyaev writes: "Vengeance is hideous but it is not for those whose wrongs have produced it to denounce its hideousness." "The disease of the revolution can never be cured by counter-revolutionaries and reactionaries. Both they and the revolutionaries live in a world of falsity and self-deception." *The Destiny of Man,* page 265.

paganism and to totalitarian control of the Church is not to be measured by the attitude of the leaders of the Church toward the war. Obedience to the state in time of war is too deeply ingrained in Christians in Germany to be affected even by their attitude toward the religious policy of the government. The well-known views of Pastor Martin Niemoeller are evidence for this. Support of a war that seems to people outside of Germany to be a war of conquest does not mean that the brave minority in the German Churches—Protestant and Catholic—which has refused to compromise on the issues which it has deemed essential has at last sold out to the state. There is, however, much evidence that the support of the war by Christians who have opposed the Church policy of the Nazis has been reluctant. It may well prove to be true that in safeguarding the center of the message of the Church from perversion Christians in Germany have done the one thing needful. Thousands of them have done it at the cost of concentration camp or complete economic insecurity. When the existing barriers have been lifted Christians outside of Germany will find a basis of fellowship with those who have preserved a central Christian loyalty. We must expect a period of tragic misunderstandings which result from the fact that Christians in Germany and those outside have not been able to confront the same facts.

From what I have learned of the spirit of the minority in the German Church which has maintained this Christian center we can regard the following letter as representative of that spirit. It was written after the beginning of the present war by a German to an

English friend with whom he had worked in the ecumenical movement:

"With these lines I have to say farewell to you. We have to expect to be called for military service in Germany. What this means for men like ourselves, who were blessed in these years of friendship and trust, by fellowship and love of Christians all over the world, that cannot now be expressed in words. . . . And now we have to go the way into darkness. We are not alone on this way. Jesus Christ is being with us. And if the day comes when the light of God and His mercy will shine again upon our peoples and Churches, then do remember, my dear friend, if I am still alive, that there is a friend of yours in whose heart all the spiritual heritage of thirteen years, does not fade away, and who will be ready for all the work of God after this time of great temptation."[15]

The Roman Church has had an ambiguous record as an institution in these times, but it has much to its credit. Both the present Pope and his predecessor have stood against anti-Semitism and overt paganism. Their record would have been better if they had not for so long regarded Communism as the one great enemy of Christianity and overlooked the menace of National Socialism and Fascism. If the worst disintegration should come over Europe, the Catholic Church would stand as the chief representative of universal values. As it is, such noble voices as those of Cardinal Faulhaber and Jacques Maritain have stood for a prophetic form of Christianity under great difficulties and such religious orders as the Benedictines

[15] *The Christian News-Letter,* November 1, 1939.

have kept alive within the Church an ethical mysticism that will inspire men in their struggle for liberty, justice, and peace.

The most that we can say about the Church when it has been under fire is that there have been minorities and remnants within it which have stood their ground. No more can be expected in view of what I have called the inflated constituency of the Church before the beginning of this pressure. But we find these minorities and remnants in all parts of the world, in Korea, for example, as well as in Europe; we can be confident that there is here the basis for new life for the Church. We can also be confident that in addition to the minorities and remnants there are vast numbers of Christians who, when the worst pressures and misunderstandings have been lifted, will respond to this vital and tested Christian witness.

2. A second reason for believing that a reformation is taking place is that there has been an extraordinary development of a social conscience within large sections of the Church during the past few decades. It is true that this development is to be found among the leaders of the Church rather than among the rank and file, among the clergy more than among the laymen. But it is of great importance for the future that so great a change has come in the leadership of the Church. Resolutions passed by a single Church council may not mean a great deal, but it is significant that for thirty years there has been a steady stream of resolutions and pronouncements on social issues from literally hundreds of Church councils. Year after year local, state, national and ecumenical Church bodies

continue to give expression to this growing Christian conscience concerning society.

A change of climate pervades the Churches. The Protestant Churches in this country have their greatest strength among the middle classes and yet a very important section of the leadership of those Churches openly identifies itself with the aspirations of other groups and is ashamed of the extent to which the Church as an institution is responsive to the middle classes. As Professor Arthur Holt says, these leaders are too urban-minded in their concentration on the cause of industrial labor, but that concentration has helped to correct their middle-class bias.[16] Protestant denominations are national in scope, but they are striving to detach themselves from narrow nationalism and at least their leaders are conscious of membership in a world Church.

Theological seminaries which train the future leadership of the Church are more alert than the Churches themselves to the social demands of Christianity.

[16]Notice this striking statement in a report presented to the Federal Council of Churches by a representative committee in 1936: "The leaders of the local Protestant churches, particularly of those which have largest influence, do not belong to that stratum of the American people [to the lower sixty percent as far as income is concerned]. They are likely to look, and very often do look, with hesitation and fear upon the struggle of the masses for better conditions of life. With this hesitation and fear they are not in a position to give the masses the moral leadership that should be available to them today within the fold of the Christian Church." It is a sign of an awakening of the conscience of the Church that such a thing as that should be said by the responsible leadership of the Protestant Churches in America.

Church boards that plan the missionary and educational enterprises of the denominations in many cases reflect this awakened social conscience. The same may be said of our most influential religious periodicals. The Federal Council of Churches embodies in large areas of its program this same concern. Missionaries and missionary executives are awake to the social needs of the nations to which missionaries are sent. Much of the leadership of the Church is critical of society and it is also critical of the Church because of its record of complacency in the face of the evils of economic injustice, racial discrimination, and war. These are all general statements which are true, in varying degrees, of individuals and institutions. The change of climate to which I point is so pervasive that those who are aware of it need no evidence for it and yet that such a change could have taken place comes as so great a surprise to those who have rejected the Church that no amount of evidence within the compass of this chapter would be enough.[17]

For reasons that are suggested in Chapter IV this social conscience of the Church must be related less directly to particular programs and movements than was the case in the days of the greatest influence of the

[17]These pronouncements until 1928 are collected in F. Ernest Johnson's *The Social Work of the Churches.* Since that time the stream of pronouncements has continued and as a result of the depression the criticisms of the economic order have become more radical. The reports of the ecumenical conferences of Oxford and Madras show the same concern. One of the most remarkable evidences of this social conscience in the Church is a document entitled: *Men, Money and the Ministry* (Longmans, 1937), signed by many bishops and clergy together with some laymen of the Church of England calling for a complete economic reform

liberal social gospel. Today the task of the Church is to develop among its own people a mind that understands the social implications of Christianity and which seeks to make social decisions intelligently in the light of the Christian social perspective. If we cannot change the mind of the constituency of the Church, we cannot change the mind of the world. I am suggesting no return to an individualistic gospel, but rather a strategy that should provide more effectively the moral support that is necessary for social change. All encouragement should be given to pioneering groups which, driven by their Christian faith, work for a more Christian society through particular movements and programs.[18]

In the minds of many the test of the reality of this change of climate will be found in the attitude of the Churches toward this war, especially the attitude of the British Churches now and the attitude of the American Churches if we become involved as a na-

---

of the Church. It outlines a plan for the pooling of resources and the fixing of an equitable scale of stipends adjusted to family needs for the clergy. The purpose of this plan is that the Church may set an example of justice within its own fellowship. The remarkable conference that met at Malvern in January, 1941, under the leadership of the Archbishop of York in order to plan for the life of the Church and the nation after the war indicates how much momentum there is behind this tendency in the Church of England.

[18]The strategy which I have in mind has been well outlined in the report of the Section on The Church and the Economic Order of the Oxford Conference. The author was the secretary of that Section. This report may be found in the *Official Report of the Oxford Conference* published by Willett and Clark (1937) or in pamphlet form from The Universal Christian Council, 297 Fourth Ave., New York City.

tion. If my argument on the limitations of pacifism as a social strategy in a previous chapter is sound, what the Church should do in time of war becomes less clear than it was to many of us five years ago. But there is ground for believing, on the basis of the present experience of the British Churches and of the present attitudes of the responsible leadership of the American Churches, that the Churches will not in any case identify uncritically the sanctities of the Christian religion with the national cause. The position which I have called Christian non-pacifism is one that the Churches can accept without surrendering to nationalism and to the madness of the war spirit.

It is significant that the major American denominations have recognized the rights of their members who are conscientious objectors to the draft on religious grounds. So do the Churches in Britain. This is a sign of the change in the attitude of the Churches toward war. It is of great importance that they hold their ground on this point in order to keep faith with the young people who have become pacifists under the influence of teaching within the Church, in order to make clear that pacifism is a genuine Christian way, in order to discipline the Churches themselves, for no Church that goes out of its way to honor and protect the conscientious objectors among its members is in much danger of losing its Christian perspective on war.

3. Since the first World War there has been a theological revival which is another ground for hope. Some of the readers of this book may question this because they tend to identify that revival with the irrational excesses of Barthianism. But in earlier chapters I have

tried to indicate many elements in the post-war theology that represent a gain in Christian insight. We are now facing a deeper layer of problems than was the case ten years ago and we are prepared once more to orient our minds toward the distinctive contribution of the Hebrew-Christian tradition. The more recent theological developments should prepare our minds too for this time of crisis; they should prevent us from identifying Christianity with social movements which in the end would pervert it or betray it. One finds the emphasis upon the conviction that God transcends all our programs and ideals—keeping the best of them under judgment—in thinkers who are as far apart as Karl Barth and Henry Nelson Wieman. I doubt if the Church as a whole has yet a crystallized message that is adequate for our times, but the materials for such a message are at hand. As I have said before,[19] this message in the hands of most of the leaders of theological thought would be relevant to the problems of civilization.

4. One of the chief grounds for belief in what I call the reformation in the Church is the trend toward unity. We find ourselves reversing the tendencies of four hundred years. For centuries it was the custom, whenever Christians differed, to separate and form a new denomination. Today when Christians differ they seek to preserve fellowship in the same Church. They are no longer tempted to use the power of the state against each other, or to anathematize each other. We see this new trend most significantly in the consciousness of membership in an ecumenical Church

[19]See page 75.

which includes the denominations, and in the development of agencies of cooperation such as the Federal Council of Churches and the World Council of Churches. We see it also in the movement toward the actual merger of denominations. There is a unity in fact now—even while we are still divided. For the most part, the leaders of the American denominations read the same books and the same periodicals; they are engaged in many cooperative enterprises locally and nationally; they can unite in preaching the gospel to the nation as in the National Preaching Mission.

To illustrate the same tendency on a world scale, I may point to the fact that it is the testimony of those who have attended the great ecumenical conferences —Oxford, Edinburgh, Madras, Amsterdam—that they felt there was a common Christianity shared by the most diverse groups which was more important than all differences. This ecumenical experience is a fact to which thousands of Christians—many of them critical in their habit of mind—can bear witness. It has been tested on a variety of occasions. It is a fact which should determine our thinking about the Church even if we have to accept it on the testimony of others.

This trend toward unity is very favorable to the development of a Church that is more Christian and more effective. But, when I say this, it is important to go on to say that unity in itself is no panacea, as enthusiastic advocates of unity often seem to think. If unity. must be bought at the price of uniformity, if it leads to the stifling of prophetic minorities or the curtailment of theological freedom it will be necessary for groups of Christians to revolt against the ecclesiastical authority of the united Church, and the process of splitting and then reuniting will be begun all over again. What one actually finds within the present trend toward unity is that it is accompanied by the will to preserve freedom. The kind of ecumenical Church to which present developments point is a Church which preserves within itself representative democracy. Doctor William Adams Brown emphasizes this as a contribution to democracy in the world. This is true of the plans for the World Council of Churches. This is true of such significant proposals for organic unity as the scheme for Church union in England.[20] Today there is actual unity in spirit and in many cooperative efforts.

The next step is obviously a kind of federation that preserves the autonomy of the cooperating Churches. Any steps beyond that will be taken very slowly and there is not the slightest evidence now of any desire to set up a vast ecclesiastical machine which will grind out uniformity. It is doubtless a great aid to the development of a form of unity which does not impose uniformity that the great Anglican Communion has succeeded in accomplishing this in its own ecclesiastical sphere. A further safeguard is that Churches which have a congregational polity are included in the

[20]See *Christendom,* Autumn 1937. This proposal will not be adopted in its present form, but that it should be presented under such high ecclesiastical auspices is quite extraordinary. It shows clearly that those who think in terms of a united Church are committed to the preservation of much flexibility and essential liberties. This scheme gives a very important place to laymen in the united Church. The Archbishop of York was the chairman of the Anglican section of the committee.

World Council of Churches. Rigid congregationalism is hardly compatible with effective unity in any form, but the concern of the Churches which have that polity to magnify the responsibility of the local Church, to give a large voice to laymen, to emphasize spiritual and intellectual freedom will protect the democratic character of any united Church. Also, I believe that all who are concerned to promote unity but who fear the possibility of too great uniformity must be thankful for the Quakers. A united Church which does not include them will always seem absurd in its pretensions and a united Church of which they are a part will preserve its freedom.

5. The fifth reason for fresh hope for the Church today is related to this new ecumenical consciousness. It is the fact that the Church is now present as an indigenous movement in every region in the world. The Church is truly a world Church for the first time as the result of the work of Christian missions. In most countries the Church is a small minority, but we can gain some idea of the importance of such a minority when we realize how much Americans are afraid of the power of a minority that they call a "fifth column." It can be said today, as it often is said, that the world Church is the only movement which has roots in all countries and which points to and mediates the sources of redemption. We can be thankful that this unification of the Church on a world scale—both in terms of a common consciousness and in terms of the development of channels of communication and cooperation—reached its present stage before the second World War began. Now, even in

this broken world, we can preserve these channels and this consciousness of belonging to the world Church, but it would be impossible now to develop them. This ecumenical communication and this fellowship may be driven underground, but I believe that they will continue to exist.[21]

In the first chapter I emphasized the role that the American Churches must play in the world Church. We have everything external in our favor. We may suffer from the lack of persecutions but at least we can use our external advantages to strengthen the Church everywhere, adding to the responsibility that we now have for the Churches in Asia and Africa a new responsibility for the aiding of the stricken and sometimes silent Churches of Europe. In the area of political decisions we are baffled and there is division among us. But there need be no division here. We can unite in saying that the strengthening of the world Church is more important than anything we may feel called upon to do on the political level, for we know that by this means we will preserve and perhaps increase resources for the new world that must come as men are driven by the dread results of war and tyranny

[21]The meaning of the world Church has been vividly presented by Henry P. Van Dusen's *For the Healing of the Nations* and Kenneth S. Latourette's *Toward a World Christian Fellowship*. The Madras Conference dramatized the fact of the world Church more fully than any other world conference because the Churches of Asia and Africa had as many representatives as those of Europe and America. It has often been said that the strongest delegation in the Conference, strongest from the point of view of their intellectual contribution and their gifts of leadership, was the delegation from China. That should help us to realize that Christianity is not merely the religion of the West.

to seek ways of organizing their common life which are closer to the intention of God.

A NOTE ON CHAPTER FIVE

I want to insert here a note on a subject to which one could not do justice even in a volume. I think that I should indicate the implications of the general point of view of this book for our thinking about the relation between the Hebrew-Christian movement and the highest levels of insight and religious living outside the Hebrew-Christian movement. Many people write —and I fear that these chapters have not been free from this tendency—as though humanity had no history outside of Europe and Palestine before the discovery of America. It appears to me that those who rule out in advance any continuity between Christianity and other religions in order to preserve the inner consistency of their own dogma of revelation are placing shackles upon God. On the other hand, it is equally apparent that those who stress the conviction that Christianity is the fulfillment of the non-Christian religions often gloss over the real differences between the Hebrew-Christian interpretation of life and, for example, the pantheistic religions. I can see no compromise between the Hebrew-Christian understanding of the worth of the historical process with its emphasis upon the righteousness of God as relevant to that process and the Hindu view that this process from an ultimate perspective lacks importance if not reality. The problem is complicated in real life by the fact that Hinduism is so tolerant and flexible that it can reinterpret itself in forms that are not incompatible with the Christian world view. That tolerance is in one context a danger because it permits a rank growth of superstitious rites, but it is also a source of opportunity because it makes possible the development of Hinduism from within.

There are elements of genuine revelation outside the Hebrew-Christian religion. If there were not, we should have to face the problem of evil in a more staggering form than is even now the case. One can put the conviction of Socrates and Plato that it is better to suffer injustice than to inflict injustice beside the ethic of Christianity and one can add that in the case of Socrates at least the teaching was embodied in a life. One can also see that the rejection of selfish desire by all of Buddhist teaching and the commandment of positive love by much Buddhist teaching—a commandment embodied in the life of the Buddha himself—are confirmations of aspects of the Christian ethic.

Even more important is the fact that there are at least two great affirmations common to almost all the great religions. These affirmations are: first, that the highest object of supreme devotion is one with ultimate reality, that God is the "determiner of destiny," as James B. Pratt has phrased it, that "What is highest in spirit is deepest in nature" to use the words of W. P. Montague. The other affirmation is that men who fulfill the conditions can find salvation; they and their aspirations are not alien to what is ultimately real in the universe. However, there is a great variety of views concerning what is highest in spirit and what is deepest in nature and there is a great variety of views concerning the conditions which men must fulfill and concerning the nature of the salvation that they can expect. Nearly all, if not all, the historical religions are a confirmation of the Christian faith in contrast to religious humanism and in contrast to the forms of naturalism which reduce the real world to the subject matter of physics and chemistry. But while there are these elements of continuity between Christianity and non-Christian religions there are points of contrast which are of great importance, which demand decisions from every human soul aware of the alternatives. There is one further consideration. There seems to be little doubt that of all the great historical religions Christianity is the only one with sufficient vitality to meet the challenge of the new political forms of paganism, to bring the world back to the worship of the God of all humanity who wills for us a community of love.

I have no faith in theological or ecclesiastical fences to emphasize the uniqueness or finality of Christianity. The uniqueness of Christianity will stand out whenever it meets other religions and Christianity will not be made more unique by having that uniqueness set up as a dogma to be accepted apart from the evidence. The finality of Christianity will depend upon its surviving the test of honest comparison with all real alternatives, comparison in the extent to which it provides illumination and power for human living under all conditions. I believe that it will survive those tests, but it would be no mistake for me to be a Christian now if at some distant time Christianity should be superseded by a religion which preserves what is valid in Christianity in the same way in which Christianity preserves what is valid in Judaism. I know that Christianity will not be superseded by a religion which places power above love or which exalts a tribal God. Whatever the future may have in store the movement with which this last chapter deals will be continued as the movement of redemption.

APPENDIX

THE PROBLEM OF EVIL

I have added this appendix to expand the thought of Chapter Two at the point at which many of us feel the most acute problem—the contrast between the pervasiveness of evil and the Christian faith in God. This is the most acute theoretical problem for theology. It is also for many souls the source of the most formidable obstacle to the Christian life. On the other hand it is important to realize that if there were no evil, our lives would have nothing to jar them from an attitude of self-sufficiency and so the absence of evil would also be a formidable obstacle to the Christian life. I need not say that the most that we can do in this area is to reduce the area in which the problem of evil is insoluble. In these days it is helpful to know that what we can say about this problem throws more light on the evil that comes into the world through human choices than the evil that has only natural causes. This appendix was written in calmer days and published as an independent article in the *Journal of Religion* for October, 1938. There are a few minor revisions and additions.

THE PROBLEM OF EVIL

THERE are two directions in which we can look for light on the problem of evil within the framework of the Christian faith in God. The first direction is suggested by any factors which we can discover in experience which condition the activity of God in the world. In so far as it is true that God's activity is so limited, it can be said that there are evils in the world which God does not will and of which God is only indirectly the cause. The second direction is suggested by any facts which we can discover in experience which indictate that some forms of evil enter into the formation of a larger good, or are the natural by-products of a structure of things which is in itself the necessary condition of a larger good. The actual evils concerning which we can get light from these two directions of our thought overlap; but we do have here two different approaches to the problem which can be discussed separately. It must not be thought that, when we have said the most that can be said along either of these lines, we have solved the problem of evil. But it can be said that the light from both of these sources may be sufficient to enable us to go on in the face of inexplicable tragedy and frustration without rebellion or cynicism or despair.

FACTORS BY WHICH THE ACTIVITY OF GOD IS CONDITIONED

Christian theology has not usually assumed the unconditioned omnipotence of God, a conception of omnipotence to which no choice among possibilities is necessary but for which all conceivable possibilities, no matter how much they contradict one another, are eternally open. The main line of Catholic theology, represented by Thomas Aquinas, definitely recognizes that the omnipotence of God is limited to those possibilities which are consistent with one another. There is a tendency to ascribe a more arbitrary kind of omnipotence to God in Calvinism, but that is not carried through to the end. It is limited chiefly to rhetoric or to the discussion of the mysteries which are beyond human understanding but which are not incompatible with the eternal righteousness and self-consistency of God. The whole Calvinistic theory of revelation is based upon faith in the self-consistency of the Holy Spirit Who does not "change His likeness" and witnesses in the heart of the believer to the same truth which He utters in the Bible. It is difficult to see how any view of the activity of God which takes seriously the temporal process at all could fail to recognize important limits to the possibilities which are open to God. The determinate character of creation means that God must deal with the world as it is and not as it might have been created. Whether in the choice of possibilities in creation God was limited by a logical structure of reality eternally confronting Him or whether He was limited by the structure of His own nature is a matter for speculation which does not greatly influence our judgment at this point about the problem of evil.

We come to the heart of the discussion of the conditions which limit the activity of God when we emphasize the fact of the freedom of finite creatures to resist the will of God. It is one of the clearest characteristics of creation that it has brought forth finite wills which are free. The nature of their freedom is a mystery, whether it be couched in terms of the mystery of indeterminism or in terms of the mystery of the self-determinism of a creative self. The range of this freedom may be subject to debate. Certainly, it is not equally distributed among human persons. Countless persons may in most areas of their lives be slaves of external circumstances, but into the molding of those circumstances have gone the free choices of other persons. The important point is not to show the precise limits of freedom but to insist that there is in the process enough human freedom to introduce a recalcitrant factor into human life which God in the exercise of an unconditioned omnipotence does not override. This human recalcitrance we know in ourselves and see its consequences everywhere. Whether or not a similar recalcitrance can be attributed to subhuman creatures as an explanation of disease and natural evil is less clear. Certainly in that case we cannot explain the existence of such recalcitrance as a by-product of the freedom which is necessary for the development of moral personality. Whether or not a similar recalcitrance can be attributed to superhuman finite spirits

—angels or devils—is a question which we can answer with only a guess. We have no convincing evidence concerning such spirits.

When we ask why God created free spirits, capable of resisting Him, instead of puppets of the divine power, perfect in their behavior, the answer is clear enough. It is familiar and need not be labored here. No writer has put it in more telling fashion than John Oman, whose *Grace and Personality*[1] is an elaboration of the theme that no form of irresistible grace can be harmonized with the conditions which are necessary for the growth of moral persons.

But there is a more difficult question: Why should the nature of man be weighted in favor of evil? In other words: Why should sin be in the line of least resistance?

The idea of the fall has been the classical Christian answer to the question concerning the tendency of sin to be in the line of least resistance. But that doctrine, as an explanation of evil, has really been no more than an evasion of the problem, either by pushing out of sight into the remote past God's most arbitrary act or by interpreting Adam's will in terms of the most impossible indeterminism or by resorting to both methods of explanation depending on whether that which was in mind was the sovereignty of God or man's responsibility for sin.[2]

The only explanation of the origin of sin which

[1]John Oman seems to be known in this country chiefly for his *The Natural and the Supernatural,* but *Grace and Personality* is probably his more distinctive contribution to theology.

[2]*Cf.* Calvin, *Institutes,* Book III, 23:7 and Book II, 1:10.

seems to me to be even plausible is that which is set forth by F. R. Tennant in his book, *The Origin and Propagation of Sin*. The following passage summarizes his position which at least throws light on the problem:

> "Instead of resorting to a hypothetical previous existence or extra temporal self decision, can we find the ground of the possibility and occasion for sin in our normal natural constitution regarded as the perfectly normal process of development through which the race has passed previously to the acquisition of full moral personality; and can we assign the rise of evil itself simply to the difficulty of the task which has to be encountered by every individual person alike, the task of enforcing his inherited organic nature to obey a moral law which he has only gradually been able to discern?" [p. 81].

There are two points which should be clarified in connection with this position. The first is that there is no conflict between this explanation of the origin of sin and the idea that sin is a permanent aspect of the human situation and that it may even take more terrible forms in combination with what seem to be higher spiritual and social developments. If we emphasize the evolutionary origin of sin in the history of the race, we may be tempted to think that sin is merely an anachronism which will in time be outgrown. But if we take the second part of the quotation from Tennant, the emphasis is upon the development of sin in the life of every child. Looked at from that point of view, this explanation of the origin of sin is consistent with the realistic recognition of the persistence of sin through all social development. Tennant enlarges upon this aspect of the problem in another paragraph:

> "Of course such a pure little animal as the young child presents sometimes an appalling spectacle of self-centredness in the satisfaction of its impulses and appetites, and of passionate resentment to restraint on their indulgence. But if the upholder of the doctrine of a fallen nature sees in such an exhibition that false delight in freedom which is said to be one of the marks of inborn depravity, the naturalist sees there only a sign of future sanity and vigor. . . . The apparent faults of infantile age are in fact organic necessities."[3]

The second point is suggested by a criticism which von Hügel applies to Tennant. He concedes that Tennant has explained the origin of the sins of appetite but claims that he has not explained the origin of the sins of pride and self-centeredness.[4] Here again it seems to me the difficulty is that von Hügel is thinking of the evolution of the race. Is it not true that the child's traits, which are the raw material of mature strength and character, are equally the raw material of pride and self-centeredness? And, during stages in which innocence and moral guilt can hardly be separated, do they not get a head start in our lives in terms of pride and self-centeredness? It is not difficult to see the reason for the origin of evil tendencies in human life; nor is it difficult to see the hazards in the way of outgrowing them or transmuting them—always under the tutelage of adults who at best have imperfectly over-

[3]*Ibid.*

[4]Baron F. von Hügel, *Essays and Addresses on the Philosophy of Religion* (1st ser.; London: J. M. Dent & Sons, 1924), p. 10.

come the same hazards. When we read in the pages of Calvin about the ruin in our nature created by Adam's fall, we must wonder that so many people develop as well as they do. But does one not have a similar experience in reading the pages of contemporary psychologists who emphasize the hazards which confront normal growth in infancy? There is at least an important element of truth in these psychological theories which gives further support for Tennant's theory of the origin of sin.

There is a second question which must be asked: Why should the tragic aspects of moral evil be compounded by aspects of human finiteness which cannot be explained as the necessary conditions for the development of moral personality? I refer to the inertia, narrowness, and stupidity of finite minds; to the limited imagination, which in combination with human egoism, turns large-scale social groups in their relations with one another into instruments of deviltry; and to the general inadequacy of the human mind in dealing with the complex and quickly changing problems of civilization. One sees the same combination of moral failure and blindness on a small scale in family life, where in the relations between parents and children the best intentions are often sadly mistaken and lead to harmful consequences for the emotional development of the children.

The only answer which can be given to this question is an extension of the answer which was given to the question about the origin of the strong tendency toward moral failure. Both the moral and the mental inadequacy of men can be traced to the general fact that in the evolution of the individual and in that of the race we have a process of growth from the lowliest beginnings. This growth is always precarious and uneven. But we know nothing of moral and mental development except as products of this kind of growth. We know of no such thing as a high spiritual result which comes to us without long, costly, and always precarious preparation. Just as moral growth comes from the transmuting of tendencies which are the materials of sin and which, in what may be called their semi-innocent stages, get a head start as the kind of behavior which is sin, so mental development is based upon trial and error in dealing with problems without which our minds would not be sharpened at all but which are not nicely adjusted so that they are always within the reach of the minds called upon to solve them. Whatever be the nature of the divine control of this process of development, it seems clear that the process has some measure of independence. I mean by this, that our sins and failures have their own inexorable chain of consequences and that we cannot expect God to intervene and break that chain. There are divine forces in the world, especially in connection with the life and death of Christ, which can break such chains, but only in so far as those who are directly involved yield themselves to God and become His instruments. The very social interdependence which makes the chain of consequences so tragic in its effects upon the innocent is itself a necessary condition for those relationships of love and fellowship without which none of the higher developments of life would be possible.

All these facts point to one conclusion which is to me inescapable.[5] It is that God, because of His own nature, faces limited possibilities. Among them are at least the following suggested by the foregoing discussion: God cannot have a world of moral persons who are not also free to resist Him. God cannot create a world of persons with either moral character or intel-

[5]I realize that this kind of argument seems blasphemous to many Christians. It appears to set our categories of reason and morality above God. With Paul they ask: "Who art thou that repliest against God?" and they usually forget that later in his discussion Paul could not allow this idea of God for whom moral standards are irrelevant to be the last word and he pushed through to the faith that in spite of appearances God would have mercy upon all (Rom. 9:20, 11:32). To say that God completely transcends our moral standards is to exalt sheer power and to empty the idea of God of the moral content that is taken for granted in the Bible. God as revealed in Christ has a definite character to be understood in terms of goodness that does not transcend completely what men think of as goodness. Religious trust will accept what comes as within the control of God in the sense that through it God can work for good but it need not assume that everything that happens is directly willed by God. In humility and against a background of mystery we must ask how the facts of horror and frustration and sin are to be harmonized with the nature of God as revealed in Christ. Readers who think that we should never say "God cannot" may well ask themselves if they really believe that God can do the precise things that are suggested in the text, since they can hardly deny that creation has a determinate character which conditions everything that is done within it.

A brilliant and provocative statement of the opposition to the attempt to deal in this way with the problem of evil is to be found in Professor Joseph Haroutunian's *Wisdom and Folly in Religion*. His pages are a needed corrective when we become too confident of our explanations of the ways of God, but it is an important commentary on his position that Professor Haroutunian believes that it leads him to the affirmation of double predestination.

ligence except by means of the slow process of development which inevitably involves all the hazards and handicaps which have been suggested. God cannot create an interdependent community of persons which is the basis of all love and fellowship without having at the same time a world in which evils spread and in which our sins and failures have incalculable consequences for the innocent. Why does God confront this limitation of possibilities? Is it not enough to say that God limited Himself? Why was it necessary for God to limit Himself when to do so meant the vast waste of the evolutionary process? What we are saying here is the same thing which Gilson says in interpreting medieval philosophy when he asserts that for God to have made creatures who were not mutable would be as impossible as it would be for Him to make round squares.[6] The bitterness of it all is somewhat covered up by that abstract word "mutable," but the same principle is involved. If there is a pattern of possibilities which is given, which includes the logical structure of reality that has often been recognized by theologians as given in this way, but which includes more that can be read only from the facts of our experience, then we can get some dim understanding of a large part of the evil from which men suffer. When we ask what the relation is between this given pattern of possibilities and God, I think that Professor Brightman puts the answer well when he says:

> "If the Given is external to God, then either he created it or he did not. If he did create it, one needs something within the divine nature to explain why he

[6]E. Gilson, *The Spirit of Medieval Philosophy*, page 120.

should create that sort of thing. If he did not create it, the presence of two ultimate powers in the universe—God and the Given—raises the problem of their interrelation and engenders many of the difficulties to which other forms of dualism are subject."[7]

I have applied this principle of the limitation of the possibilities between which God must choose only to those forms of evil which come into the world through human agency. That the same principle must be extended to cover all of nature I am prepared to believe, but I have no confidence in saying how it should be done. Except in the case of the effect of the obviously necessary regularities of nature upon human life, where it can be said that God could not have at the same time both the order on which all higher developments depend and a world which would be accident-proof, it is not clear how we are to think of the relation of nature to the continuous creative and guiding activity of God, on the one hand, and to human suffering, on the other. All speculations which trace disease to the "freedom" of the germs as they trace sin to the freedom of man neglect the fact that in the case of human freedom we do see a relationship between it and a high result which is worth the cost. In the case of the germs we may hypothesize a similar freedom, but let us not be fooled into thinking that the use of the word carries with it even an approximate solution of the

[7]E. S. Brightman, *The Problem of God,* page 183. Professor Brightman in his conception of the "Given" includes more than I am suggesting here, but his general argument that the recognition that God confronts limitations involves us in the dilemma which he outlines seems to me to be sound.

problem. The only clear light which we can get on the human suffering which is the work of nature must come from the second approach to the problem of evil to which we shall soon turn. In this connection it is important to take to heart the warning that we must not think of the purposes of God as concerned exclusively with the welfare of man.

This first approach gives us chiefly understanding of the evil which comes into the world through human agency. It does illumine not only individual cases of sin and frustration but also the social catastrophes which weigh so heavily on our minds in these days. Our generation needs light upon social catastrophes, and such light theology has less difficulty in giving than it has in the case of natural evil. And yet I think that it is true that social evil which can be more easily explained is more likely to give us a sense of the complete meaninglessness of existence than natural evil which, though a greater mystery, is so often borne with deepened faith.

EVIL AS A PART OR CONDITION OF GOOD

There are many facts which indicate that evil can be explained in part as an element in a larger good, as a condition of good, or as the by-product of a structure of things which is itself a condition of good. This approach to the problem is less controversial than the first. All Christian thinkers would admit the importance of these facts. They would differ on the extent to which these facts represent a solution of the problem of evil. It may be said in general that in the kind of world in which we live it is better that there should be evil—evil as it is taken up and made into the stuff of character and spiritual life, evil as it is overcome by divine and human acts of redemption, evil as it is known in contrast with good. This general explanation is not to be brought out on all occasions as an explanation of specific evils which, so far as we can see, contribute to no good. Nor is it to be used as an excuse for tolerating evils; "God forbid!" as Paul said when it was suggested that he taught that we should sin that grace may abound. Evil that is kept alive for the sake of these by-products of good will be evil only to those who are responsible for it. From some perspectives the death of Christ was the condition of good, but it did no good to Judas, and Caiaphas, and Pilate.

The first type of evil which can be explained in relation to good is that which is not in itself a part of a larger good but which is a by-product of a condition of things which is necessary for the realization of good. The simplest illustration is to be found in the case of accidents. They are a particularly poignant form of evil, partly because they are so sudden and catch us unprepared, partly because they seem avoidable, and partly because we can so easily imagine ourselves or those closest to us in the situation of the accident. And yet, there is no form of evil which is more readily explained and harmonized with the love and power of God. Given the regularities of nature, the facts which underlie the law of gravitation, the fact that fire can be depended on to burn—regularities without which there could be no character, no learning, no cumulative human achievement—and given human fallibility as well as human sin, we can say that, while no particular accident may be necessary, it is statistically inevitable that there will be accidents.

Human qualities which we value most can hardly be thought of as possible at all without evil or at least the strong possibility of evil; without evil or the strong possibility of evil there would be no such thing as courage or compassion or tested loyalty. The deeper levels of all virtues, of all human fellowship, cannot be imagined in our kind of world without evil. Here it is clearest that the evil is not to be kept alive in order that we may develop these qualities. They are real only as they involve the struggle to overcome evil. If there is the least suggestion that evil is being kept alive in order to make us the more courageous and compassionate, the qualities which do result are sentimental counterfeits. I do not know whether or not it is possible under conditions which we have not experienced to have human character reach its highest development without evil to overcome. I do know that in any human society in which there are still sin and death and many maladjustments between man and nature and in which every generation has to face afresh all the problems of growing up there still will be evil enough for our good.

There is also the disciplinary effect of suffering. This is somewhat different from the evil which is really the occasion of particular human qualities. It is the effect of suffering upon the total personality. It is easy to be sentimental about this and overlook the degree to which suffering crushes, embitters, numbs the soul, or drives souls insane. The greatest mystery of all is why some souls are able to transmute evil into good in their own lives and others are shattered by it. But, when we have said all this, it still remains true that without suffering life is lived on a superficial level; we become self-sufficient, complacent, and proud. Suffering deepens and strengthens every quality which we have. It can purify us from preoccupation with trivial things. It raises love and comradeship to the highest level. It forces us out of ruts and often gives life a new beginning. So long as the soul is able to use suffering in this way it has this value; but, when in the form of mental disease suffering destroys the soul's capacity to transmute it, we have one form of evil that seems to be unqualified evil.

Then there is the relation of evil to the most meaningful events of individual life and history. This is probably not a separate point, but it does suggest a different way of looking at the same facts which we have been considering.

I want to put side by side two quotations from widely different sources. The first is what Father Tyrrell once wrote to a friend under doom of death:

> "I have long since ceased trying to explain the confusions and catastrophes of life in any coherent way. What I cling to still is the belief that most lives are justified by one or a very few moments that bring out the best in us. The rest is mere padding and sawdust. If that is not true, I do not know what to think for utilitarian standards are mere moonshine. A few hours of endeavor and endurance on the rack of the cross have an absolute value that will last when all our works are obliterated like scratching on the sand."[8]

[8]M. D. Petre, *Autobiography: Life of George Tyrrell,* Vol. II, page 428.

The second, Vanzetti's statement in the courtroom after receiving sentence:

> "If it had not been for these things, I might have such work for tolerance, for joostice, for man's undermen. I might have die, unmarked, unknown, a failure. Now we are not a failure. This is our career and our triumph. Never in our full life could we hope to do such work for tolerance, for joostice, for man's understanding of man as now we do by accident. Our words—our lives—our pains—nothing! The taking of our lives—lives of a good shoemaker and a poor fish-peddler—all! That last moment belongs to us—that agony is our triumph."[9]

It has often been pointed out—emphasized especially by Bosanquet in dealing with evil—that the world's greatest literature is tragedy. One is forced to face the question whether a world in which tragic events were impossible and in which men did not understand them would be a better or a poorer world. For the Christian it is the question of whether or not the world would be better or poorer without the cross. We know it would be poorer, and yet one must not say that, without repeating what I have already said—the cross brings redemption only to those who repent of their responsibility for it and for their share in all the processes which make men victims in our day.

THE OVERCOMING OF EVIL

Christians are quite right when they say that the practical problem of overcoming evil is of far greater

[9] *The Letters of Sacco and Vanzetti,* page v.

importance than the theoretical problem of explaining its origin and meaning in relation to the goodness and power of God. If, however, we had no light at all on its origin and meaning, we might be driven to save appearances by glossing over the facts and making evil appear good or unreal, or we might be tempted to think of God as the enemy. The practical overcoming of evil, the transmuting of evil in experience, provides data which are of great importance for the solution of the theoretical problem. If we did not see in experience evil so transmuted that it enters into a larger good, we should have no ground for citing such a tendency as one explanation of evil; and, if we did not find in life great resources for the overcoming of evil, we should not have the faith for which evil creates a problem.

The overcoming of evil which is already a part of our experience takes two forms. The first is the social meliorism by which the suffering of this present time gets part of its meaning from its consequences for good for the future. We are all casting out utopianism, but we must not cast out with it all hope for a better future—for a future in which at least men will be able to live in an interdependent world without destroying one another. We cannot expect to eliminate evil, but there is ground for belief that the forces of redemption in history are stronger than the forces of destruction and that what we do or suffer now will not be lost but in ways beyond all possibility of prediction will enter into a future good. This belief is difficult now for a generation which has suffered such profound disillusionments, and there is a serious question as to how long it can stand at all except on the basis of religious conviction. But the Christian has not only a general belief that God is at work in the world; he has seen God work most powerfully through a cross which must have seemed to those who observed it as an event in history to be the last word in human weakness; he has seen how often God has quite literally taken the weak things of the world, that He might put to shame the things that are strong.

The second form of the overcoming of evil which we experience is in the individual life. It is a fact that men, whenever they fulfill the conditions, do turn evil into good. Those who make the right adjustment to God, who by faith and loyalty and humility escape from cramping self-concern, do find evil a means of blessedness. John Oman puts the matter into relief when he states the opposite truth that "All things work for evil to those who love themselves."[10]

But, when I have said these things, I must go on to mention certain difficulties which confront us as we think of the overcoming of evil in either of these ways and as we think of the possibility of an ultimate divine victory over evil.

Difficulty in regard to social meliorism.—Professor Charles Hartshorne has written forcefully of the shortsightedness of those who refuse to face the strong probability that there can be no indefinite future for the race on this earth.[11] It is this prospect which makes nontheistic humanism really ultimate pessimism. If we think of the human race being blotted out at the

[10]*Grace and Personality,* page 117.
[11]*Beyond Humanism,* chap. II.

height of its development by a cosmic catastrophe, we must see that hopes of social meliorism do not provide adequate scope for the overcoming of evil. How much worse is the possibility that by gradual processes this planet will become unable to support human life and that men may be driven back to savagery in the final struggle over a diminishing food supply!

Difficulty in regard to the personal transmuting of evil.—Here there is a difficulty of a different kind which we cannot evade. It is true, I believe, that for those who do fulfill the conditions all external evil can be made into the means of blessedness. But there are so many who seem to be unable to fulfill the conditions. Persons are blocked by physiological or psychological or environmental conditions so that it is impossible for them to develop the spiritual strength and insight which are essential if they are to overcome evil in their own lives. What are we to say of the feeble-minded child, or of the man of great devotion who, partly because he does not spare himself, suffers a nervous breakdown and ends his life in this world in a kind of hell? Inequality in the distribution of evil handicaps and in the distribution of the power to overcome them is the hardest of all facts to face. Our fathers noted this fact and traced it either to God's eternal decree or to an abstract kind of freedom which was thought to be within the reach of every soul. Indeed, they used the horizons opened up by immortality not only to provide for some persons the joys which outweighed all temporal suffering but also to make the problem of spiritual inequality a more terrible problem; for the most part they were willing to accept the prospect that a large part of the human race would know only evil eternally.

The horizons offered by immortality do suggest the only possibility that evil will finally be overcome by God. Immortality is no short cut to a solution of our problem. For all that we know, any future existence will have its own forms of evil and its own problem of evil. Moreover, nothing could be worse than to use the idea of immortality to freeze for all time and all eternity the human distinctions which emerge among men in this short life. But immortality does provide new opportunities for the transmuting of evil by persons, new possibilities for the overcoming of evil by God. The affirmation of belief in immortality is our way of affirming in the face of these difficulties ultimate trust in God.

BIBLIOGRAPHY

BIBLIOGRAPHY

Chapter One

The first part of this chapter is based upon reflection on contemporary events as interpreted by much literature that is too scattered and ephemeral for use here. I recommend the following books as a means of introduction to the theological developments mentioned in the chapter and as the source of further bibliographical suggestions:

Aubrey, Edwin Ewart. *Present Theological Tendencies* (Harpers, 1936)
Baillie, John, and Martin, Hugh (editors). *Revelation* (Macmillan, 1937)
Horton, Walter M. *Contemporary English Theology* (Harpers, 1936)
—— *Contemporary Continental Theology* (Harpers, 1938)
Pauck, Wilhelm. *Karl Barth: Prophet of a New Christianity?* (Harpers, 1931)

Chapter Two
[and Appendix]

Baillie, John. *Our Knowledge of God* (Scribners, 1939)
Brightman, E. S. *A Philosophy of Religion* (Prentice-Hall, 1940)

Brunner, Emil. *God and Man* (Macmillan, 1936)
Calhoun, Robert L. *God and the Common Life* (Scribners, 1935)
Horton, Walter M. *God* (Association Press, 1937)
Macmurray, John. *The Clue to History* (Harpers, 1939)
Matthews, W. R. *God in Christian Thought and Experience* (Harpers, 1930)
Oman, John. *Grace and Personality* (Macmillan, 1925)
Robinson, H. Wheeler. *The Religious Ideas of the Old Testament* (Scribners, 1913)
Tennant, F. R. *Philosophical Theology* (Vol. II) (Cambridge University Press, 1930)
Van Dusen, Henry P. *God in These Times* (Scribners, 1935)

CHAPTER THREE

Aubrey, Edwin Ewart. *Man's Search for Himself* (Cokesbury, 1940)
Augustine, St. *Confessions*
Berdyaev, N. *The Destiny of Man* (Scribners, 1937)
Brunner, Emil. *Man in Revolt* (Scribners, 1940)
Calhoun, Robert L. *What Is Man?* (Association Press, 1939)
Jessop, T. E., and others. *The Christian Understanding of Man* (Willett, Clark, 1938)
Maritain, Jacques. *True Humanism* (Scribners, 1938)
May, Rollo. *The Springs of Creative Living* (Cokesbury, 1940)
Niebuhr, Reinhold. *Moral Man and Immoral Society* (Scribners, 1932)
—— *Beyond Tragedy* (Scribners, 1937)
——*The Nature and Destiny of Man,* Vol. I, *Human Nature* (Scribners, 1941)
Pascal, Blaise. *Thoughts*

Robinson, H. Wheeler. *The Christian Doctrine of Man* (Scribners, 1911)
Williams, N. P. *The Ideas of the Fall and Original Sin* (Longmans, 1929)

Chapter Four

Barth, Karl. *The Church and the Political Problem of Our Day* (Scribners, 1939)
Bennett, John C. *Social Salvation* (Scribners, 1935)
Brunner, Emil. *The Divine Imperative* (Macmillan, 1937)
Cadoux, C. J. *Christian Pacifism Re-examined* (Blackwell, 1940)
Demant, V. A. *God, Man and Society* (Morehouse, 1934)
Ehrenström, Nils. *Christian Faith and the Modern State* (Willett, Clark, 1937)
Ehrenström, N., Dibelius, M., and others. *The Christian Faith and the Common Life* (Willett, Clark, 1938)
Johnson, F. Ernest. *The Social Gospel Re-examined* (Harpers, 1940)
McNeill, John T. *The Christian Hope for World Society* (Willett, Clark, 1937)
Niebuhr, Reinhold. *An Interpretation of Christian Ethics* (Harpers, 1935)
Oldham, J. H. (editor). *The Oxford Conference—Official Report* (Willett, Clark, 1937)
Rauschenbusch, Walter. *A Theology for the Social Gospel* (Macmillan, 1922)
Scott-Craig, T. S. K. *Christian Attitudes to War and Peace* (Scribners, 1938)
Tittle, Ernest Fremont. *Christians in an Unchristian Society* (Association Press, 1939)
Woolman, John. *The Journal of John Woolman*

Chapter Five

Andrews, H. T., and others. *The Lord of Life* (Macmillan, 1929)

Brown, William Adams. *The Church: Catholic and Protestant* (Scribners, 1935)

Dodd, C. H. *History and the Gospel* (Scribners, 1939)

Horton, Walter, M. *Realistic Theology* (Harpers, 1935)

—— *Can Christianity Save Civilization?* (Harpers, 1940)

Latourette, Kenneth. S. *Toward a World Christian Fellowship* (Association Press, 1938)

—— *Anno Domini* (Harpers, 1940)

McCown, C. C. *The Search for the Real Jesus* (Scribners, 1940)

Morrison, Charles Clayton. *What Is Christianity?* (Willett, Clark, 1940)

Porter, F. C. *The Mind of Christ in Paul* (Scribners, 1930)

Oldham, J. H., and 't Hooft, Visser. *The Church and Its Function in Society* (Willett, Clark, 1937)

Van Dusen, Henry P. *For the Healing of the Nations* (Scribners, 1940)

Van Dusen, H. P., and Cavert, S. McC. *The Church Through Half a Century* (Scribners, 1936)

The World Mission of the Church (Madras Report) (International Missionary Council, 1939)

The Christian News-Letter (Editor: J. H. Oldham) (It is possible to subscribe to this weekly paper for a year by sending $3.00 to the Universal Christian Council, 297 Fourth Ave., New York City)

INDEX

INDEX

Sermon Topics

Books.